# CIRCLES
## OF
## FRIENDS

Linda —
Best wishes
Bob Penske
12-9-88

# CIRCLES OF FRIENDS

People with
Disabilities and
Their Friends Enrich the
Lives of One Another

## Written by Robert Perske
## Illustrated by Martha Perske

Abingdon Press

*Nashville*

CIRCLES OF FRIENDS

This book is printed on acid-free paper.

**Library of Congress Cataloging-in-Publication Data**

PERSKE, ROBERT.
    Circles of friends: people with disabilities and their
friends enrich the lives of one another.
    Robert Perske: illustrated by Martha Perske.
    p. cm.
    1. Handicapped—United States—Psychology—
Case studies.
    2. Friendship—Case studies. 3. Helping behavior
—Case studies. I. Title.
    HV1553.P47 1988                           88-14616
    362.4'048—dc19                                CIP

**ISBN 0-687-08390-7** (pbk.)

    The drawing on pp. 6 and 58 is reprinted with
permission of Free to Be Foundation, Inc. First
appeared in *Free to Be . . . A Family.*
    The drawing on p. 48 is reprinted with permission
of the Association for Retarded Citizens of the
United States.
    Sections from the article by Wynn DeBevoise
reprinted in Chapter 18 are from *Principal*, vol. 65,
No. 4, March 1986. Copyright 1986, National
Association of Elementary school Principals. All
rights reserved.
    Carolyn Daniel's letter reprinted in Chapter 10 is
from *Parent to Parent*, April 1987, pp. 2-3. Used with
permission.
    The drawing on p. 76 appeared on the cover of the
September 1976 issue of *Early Years.*

MANUFACTURED BY THE PARTHENON PRESS AT
NASHVILLE, TENNESSEE, UNITED STATES OF AMERICA

We dedicate this book
to
Robert Williams.

We refuse to forget the words of that forward-thinking woman in Salem, Oregon, who stood up and said, "We are tired of being seen first as handicapped, or retarded, or developmentally disabled. We want to be seen as *people first*" (Perske, 1978, p. 54). With gratitude, and in keeping with *Guidelines for Reporting and Writing About People with Disabilities* (RTC/IL), we have constructed the sentences of this book so that words like *friends, persons, people, citizens,* and *human beings* appear before the words for a disability (i.e., "a friend with a disability"). Words that describe disabilities will be used as sparingly as possible.

Justin Fandl and Spencer Hutchings

PERSKE

# Contents

# 1 - The Reason for This Book

Life isn't always fair.

Our planet contains a small number of people who *appear* to function like eagles. In childhood, their bodies and minds and senses develop with reasonable ease. In school, they warm the hearts of their teachers by rising quickly to the top of their classes. As adults, they soar and dive and compete and win at whatever they attempt. They seem to be right up there on the list for Survival of the Fittest.

But this world also contains a tiny number of people who *appear* to function like birds with short or even broken wings. Their childhood development becomes an obstacle course, and those of the old school try to avoid them as much as possible. They feel the same longings as the eagles do, but they are at a terrible disadvantage. They exert many times more energy just to climb or move ahead. And when they or their loved ones hear talk about survival of the fittest, they flinch.

As for the rest of us—the masses of ordinary people who live on this planet—our development *appears* to hover around average (sometimes above and sometimes below). And yet, powerful forces—parents, teachers, television, billboards, and who knows what else—tilt our thinking toward believing that most things worth striving for can be found up on the mountain top with the eagles. After all, if and when The Great Cut comes, we think it better to be found in a nest with those above-average people. We dread being seen as below average, even though in every competitive situation we can think of, 50 percent of us fall into that lower group.

Quite often we jump at a chance to befriend those who run fastest, hit the ball farthest, give the greatest speeches, create the best technologies, come up with the best theories, attract the most members of the opposite sex, or make the most people laugh or cry. These are the people whose faces appear frequently on magazine pages and television screens.

That's why most doors in our neighborhoods would open wide to them.

And maybe that's why—until recently—our community portals often were closed to many with severe physical, sensory, or developmental disabilities.

Fortunately, some of us now feel that continually stretching in the direction of eagles can be tiring.

We long for wisdom to make the world more decent and tolerant and caring, a world where all of us figure in one another's survival. We believe that much of the wisdom needed for this task comes from reaching toward those we may have been programmed to avoid.

· · · · ·

We found a few down-to-earth, large-hearted adults and students who became good friends with people once thought too limited or strange for life in ordinary neighborhoods. To our surprise, these friendships became our "living documents." From them we drew the stories, ideas, and images for this book. And we feel we have only scratched the surface. Come along with us.

*Robert and Martha Perske*

# 2 - All Aboard

PERSKE

*Sutherlin, Oregon,* September 16, 1987—Playmates of Susi Prince have found a fun way to get around lately—by forming a train behind Susi's electric wheelchair. And her friends returned the favor.

"Kids in the neighborhood have helped her more than anything," said Susi's mother. "They've just been great." Susi recently has undergone several surgeries related to cerebral palsy. Her mother said Susi is happy to be back in school. (Associated Press)

The drawing of Susi and her friends was made by permission of Wide World Photo. Photographer Mark Saba of the *Roseburg News-Review* captured the group in action.

# 3 - Why Friends Are Important

Friendships are such an everyday thing, we just take them for granted. They are like electricity, telephone, clothing, and three meals a day—we anguish only when we are deprived of them.

And yet we have just begun to sense the pain experienced by people with disabilities when they are deprived of mutually satisfying friendships with ordinary people. We suddenly see that family support, regular schooling, and community living programs are not enough. Those people need friends just as we do. Consider these facts:

*Friendship is a familiar but elusive term.* Alfred North Whitehead, in *Science and the Modern World*, shows that familiar things—like friendships—are the hardest to research (p. 6). Researchers, of course, reduce their focus to specific *relationships* or *social interactions*, classifying, counting, and analyzing. But the rest of us need to view a good friendship the way we look at a sunrise, seeing it in all its radiance. Otherwise, as Whitehead believes, research will degenerate into a medley of ad hoc hypotheses, truncated findings without a philosophical base (p. 25).

*Families provide things that friends can't.* We need childhood nurturing, a place in a family history, strong birth-to-death ties.

*But friends help us stretch beyond our families.* In *Just Friends*, social scientist Lillian Rubin illustrates vividly that young people turn more to friends than to family when they seek to be affirmed as adults (pp. 15-33).

*Human-service workers do things that friends can't.* When such a team is at its best, it can focus on a specific problem and draw up an orchestrated plan. Then, in unison, the workers try to help a person achieve a specific healthy outcome.

*But friends help us move beyond human-service goals.* Friends provide us with myriad options that never could be programmed.

*Friends help us rehearse adult roles.* You and I are the way we are largely because we rehearse our actions and attitudes with friends—things we wouldn't think of saying or doing with family or human-service workers.

*Friends serve as fresh role models.* We often choose certain friends because we see something in them that we wish for ourselves.

*Good friendships are a mystery.* There's no ritual or program for starting them. Sometimes they thrive and sometimes they fade. And they may end without celebration, certificate, plaque, funeral, or divorce decree.

*Good friendships are attractive.* Others watch interactions between friends with great interest.

As Letty Pogrebin, in *Among Friends*, says, "Friendship is like sex: We always suspect there's some secret technique we don't know about" (p. 5).

*Friendships generate their own energy.* Quite often, when two people do things together, their zest and success equal much more than the sum of two people's efforts.

*Friendships become a haven from stress.* When things get tough, many of us have good friends "on call."

*Spouses and committed couples can be good friends.* When two people can't, they are in trouble.

*Friendships are reciprocal.* Both parties receive enrichment from the relationship.

*People in authority often frown on friendships.* In *The Four Loves*, C. S. Lewis says, "Men who have real friends are less easy to manage or 'get at'; harder for good authorities to correct or for bad authorities to corrupt" (p. 115).

*Friends can demystify strange behaviors.* While I visited two friends in a print shop in Rockville, Maryland, one friend—during a moment of boredom—began to move his arms and fingers in patterns professionals call "autistic." When I asked the other friend what he thought about such movements, he replied, "Hey man, if you think that's weird, you should come with me to my favorite tavern on Friday nights."

*Human-service workers cannot program friendships.* They can, however, set up frameworks in which friendships can happen.

*Every friendship is unique and unrepeatable.* What happens in each relationship sets it apart as vividly as a fingerprint. That's why each friendship described in this book differs vastly from the others.

*One can learn much from good friendships.* A good friendship can become a *living document*. With great interest, we can study the remarkable things friends do with each other. And it doesn't matter whether society has imaged us as a so-called normal or as a person with a disability, good friendships can inspire us to try refreshing new interpersonal activities in our own lives—things we've never done before.

The Joshua Committee: Judith Snow, center. Right and moving clockwise: Peter Dill, Jack Pearpoint, Marsha Forest, Peter Clutterbuck, and Sandy Gray.

# 4 - Friends Circle to Save a Life

*Toronto, Ontario*—the first time we met, it took only a second before I looked past the motorized wheelchair and the rotary switch she operated with her right thumb—the only part of her body she can move below the neck. Judith Snow's deep, warm voice and her kind, round rosy-cheeked face, suddenly made me feel I was one of the most valuable people in her life. And when I looked into her eyes, I saw graciousness and an intense love of life. Later, I knew those eyes had seen more battles in her short lifetime than others might see in two long ones.

People know Judith as a no-nonsense woman capable of describing a complete situation with a single metaphor, cutting through ambiguous issues to what's *really* right and wrong. She possesses a repertoire of emotions so honest and free, she could have danced on tables. But sometimes I catch my breath when I think about a human-service system that surely would have killed her if it hadn't been for a precious circle of friends.

With a chuckle, Judith told me she came into the world in 1949, in the General Motors town of Oshawa, Ontario, "coming off the assembly line like a Monday morning product." Others must have thought so, too, judging from the many attempts to "fix" her severe muscular dystrophy, as if she really were a car:

- Physicians attempted corrective surgery in her first year of life.
- At age ten, steroid medications succeeded only in dropping her soprano voice to a bass.
- At thirteen, she underwent two radiation treatments in unsuccessful sterilization attempts. Medical personnel decided against the third; it might have killed her.
- Later an unsuccessful back operation cost her the use of her arms, except for that single thumb. And she developed a constant pain in one leg.

Physicians predicted she would be dead by age thirty. And when doctors predict . . . well, people *do* pay attention. After all, here was a person who scooted all over town in her motorized wheelchair. But when she was out of it, she depended totally on others to handle her basic needs—bathroom needs, dressing, eating, getting in and out of bed—things we take for granted. When helpers weren't *careful*, Judith paid the price in added pain. And if things were done wrong, she could have died.

Public school served as an obstacle course. Her parents, rejecting pressures to institutionalize Judith and believing she could contribute to society, moved to Whitbe, Ontario, thinking she could receive a better education there. But when she was twelve, the district refused to keep her in school, so the family moved to Pickering, Ontario. There the school accepted Judith, and her grade average climbed from C to A.

As for friends, she didn't have any, and she was kept away from places where she could have found friends.

"I learned to be a disabled person," she said. "You don't expect people to be your friends. You have a shell. And so I worked three or four hours a day on homework. It became a psychological defense."

Then came days at York University in Toronto, with the government providing much-needed attendant care. In this environment, she moved in her wheelchair from class to class—and all over metro Toronto. She soared academically, winning bachelor's and master's degrees and an academic achievement award. But most important, she suddenly began to refuse to be everybody's project, an "always-compliant crip," with everyone else making choices for her.

At graduation in 1976, things looked bright. But no one dreamed how many unfeeling, rule-worshiping government functionaries lurked in her future.

Her school-related attendant-care program dropped away, and all attempts to get that support from other agencies failed. No funds for this type of disability, they said.

At the same time, Judith founded the university's Center for Special Services for Handicapped Students, and since she had already demonstrated her natural skill as an advisor and advocate for others with disabilities, she became the first director. She often did the work of two, but her salary fell far short of one able-bodied professional's pay, making it impossible for her to cover her own attendant care.

She applied for housing and assistance at a community residence she had helped to found, but they rejected her; she was too disabled. Since other attempts had not been successful, she moved into a nursing home.

And so she exuded the perky strength of a counselor to students in crisis during the day, but returned each evening to the nursing home, where staff members viewed everyone as sick—or as belligerent. Because she arrived after supper was over, her meal consisted of a peanut butter sandwich. Care for her other needs was slipshod, and Judith suffered repeated bouts of bronchitis, skin rash, and stomach bleeding. But she weathered it all and kept going.

Then the nursing home asked her to leave. "The owners felt they weren't making enough money," she said, "even though I was gone all day. They said I was too sick to live in a nursing home."

Judith moved to a chronic-care institution where the common-denominator rules were ingrained in staff members; she had to pay a private nurse to get her up, bathed, dressed, and nourished so that she could get to work on time. Then, because a good night's sleep was impossible on the ward (many of the women screamed at night), she paid for a semiprivate room.

"I paid for the privilege of living with a 102-year-old-woman who called out loudly for nurses all day," she said. "But not at night, thank God."

At the same time, Judith's skills as a teacher had developed until professors asked her to lead class sessions and workshops on the political and social aspects of disability—though her own situation continued to deteriorate. The cold meals, staff members' inability to render regular, careful care—especially getting her to the toilet as often as she needed—slowly defeated her until she ended in the hospital, suffering from malnutrition and influenza.

When she was well, she begged human-service workers not to send her back to the institution. She asked for an alternative situation—any place where she could receive the attendant care she needed. They found nothing, and she was returned to the institution.

But she went back fighting. She demanded warm meals and the right to bathroom help when she needed it. She even persuaded a physician to write it out as an order.

But her new plan failed. All the regular aides evaded her; she was assigned only those who couldn't speak English.

As exhaustion approached again, a campus physician allowed Judith to move into a university residence for a two-week rest. She paid for attendant care, using her meager savings to hire students.

After those two weeks, she couldn't face going back to the institution, so she moved into a friend's hallway and continued to pay students to help her. She thought she only had to "get by" for five months, since she had been promised a spot in an apartment building with a brand new attendant-care program.

Later, the government official who had made the promise reneged. The new rules stated that anyone who needed more than three and a half hours of attendant care a day could not be served outside an institution.

On March 6, 1980—four days before Judith was scheduled to help lead a provincial workshop on understanding people with disabilities—she collapsed, totally exhausted. One colleague described her mental condition as "just like falling into a black hole." Another heard her say, "I can't go on. . . I can't ask anyone, anymore, to do anything else for me." After that, she spoke little and sometimes incoherently.

It suddenly became clear to her colleagues that Judith had been struggling heroically simply to stay alive. She collapsed when she was thirty, the very age limit some physicians had set for her existence.

. . . . .

Judith Snow would have been gone for good if it hadn't been for five people who circled around her, almost like firefighters preparing to catch a falling body in a net: Peter Dill, Sandy Gray, and Peter Clutterbuck of the Canadian Association for Community Living; Marsha Forest and Jack Pearpoint of Frontier College. Ironically, all worked as educators or in human services, but none of their agencies —no matter how high-sounding their goals— could give immediate help to this woman with such acute needs. So the five took off their professional coats and came together around Judith as a circle of friends.

Dill, the convener of the workshop in which Judith was to have been a speaker, first learned of her collapse. He called Forest, and together, they took her to Forest's home and put her to bed, where she stayed for a week. Then Forest and Dill called an emergency meeting.

Not mentioning mental breakdown or physical exhaustion or letting go to die, Forest opened the meeting in her clipped, optimistic manner: "Look, people, I need Judith. I need to get her back to work again." She explained to the fourteen professionals and students at the meeting that what Judith really needed was her own home and her own attendant care. Immediately, the enlarged circle came up with an emergency plan of donated time and money.

Two days later, when Judith began to talk and regain her strength, the five original circle members gathered around her and began long-range planning. They listened to what Judith wanted, and they didn't think it was unreal for her to have a home and love and a profession such as they had. On large pieces of paper taped to the wall, they listed funds available and funds needed. They developed a roster of paid and volunteer attendant-care persons. They brainstormed ways to persuade the existing human-service agencies to respond to Judith's *real* situation.

Judith, moved by what her friends had done, dubbed them the Joshua Committee—a group of people who knew how to break down walls. When the meeting ended, Judith's support system seemed stable. But nobody knew, given Judith's needs, how long that stability could last.

During the next month, the Joshua Committee spent almost every moment of free time on what was described as an impossible mess. Yet each member undertook a separate piece of action:

- Gray became round-the-clock coordinator of attendant care. When there was a gap, she filled it herself.
- Clutterbuck became the exacting builder of practical budgets and worked on proposals for raising money.
- Dill found Judith an interim apartment. He also held the quiet, intuitive belief that five persons together could mysteriously generate a power much more than each of the five separately. He was right.

- Pearpoint confronted the administrator of Ontario's Ministry of Social Services in a public workshop—a workshop that was to have included Judith, but who was still too ill to attend. Pearpoint called the official's attention to the empty chair on the platform. He spoke about Judith's condition and the broken promises of the human-service agencies. In that public meeting, the official promised the special care funds she needed, but later, he couldn't remember that promise. So the committee called a press conference—and the official's memory came back! The press conference suddenly served as an occasion to thank the official for his brilliant management of the whole affair.

- Forest, a close friend, was the tough-but-loving cheerleader for the whole group—hustling here and there, paying attention to every detail, pointing out new directions, at times even screaming at the others.

- Judith became the sixth member of the Joshua Committee, encouraged by the others to take control of her own support system as it fell into place. *Her* choices were the ones to be followed! Able-bodied people would never choose for her again! And so she became a lusty chooser, and even learned to scream! There has been a lot of screaming at Joshua Committee meetings these past seven years.

. . . . .

Today the Canadian government recognizes Judith Snow as a leading expert on the political and social situation of people with disabilities. As a consultant for the Canadian Association for Community Living, she travels the continent with well-trained, caring attendants and works long hours on behalf of others with disabilities. She calls herself a "portable visionary who tries to show others how to encircle a person in crisis." She lives in a simple apartment in a trendy Toronto neighborhood and can often be seen scooting around the neighborhood streets in her motorized wheelchair, greeting people, stopping to talk. It is safe to say she now has hundreds of friends and colleagues who have interacted or collaborated professionally with her.

The government pays for her attendant care beyond the means of her own salary, just half of what it was paying to keep her in the institution. Interestingly, the money must be sent to Frontier College, which disburses the money to her. (A government rule forbids giving cash to an individual—it can be given only to human-service systems.)

But what of the Joshua Committee members themselves? They can document more than 100 successful circles that now function throughout Ontario. Each member of the group has applied the Joshua Committee experience in a different area. Marsha Forest helps ordinary kids encircle those with disabilities in regular school classrooms. Peter Dill finds others to surround families with members having a disability. Sandy Gray develops the same kind of circle in park and recreation programs. Jack Pearpoint includes circles in his Beat-the-Street programs in downtown Toronto. Peter Clutterbuck has gone back to fiscal work, but he stands ready at the ring of a telephone to demonstrate that "successful circles of friends around a person with a disability can save governments thousands of dollars."

As for Judith Snow, she continues to look into any situation where a person is being pushed down or held back. And in June 1987, she announced her engagement to be married. See what happens when you give people choices?

Does the Joshua Committee still meet? It does, periodically. The meetings are less messy now, occasionally even boring. After all, Judith now has more than five friends, and she's in many other circles. But if a time ever comes when a human-service agency applies a mindless, unfeeling rule, the Joshua Committee will be back in business. Fast.

# 5 - Joshua Committee, You Stretch Our Vision

The Joshua Committee—vivid living document that it is—challenges us to see certain things more clearly than ever before.

Students, after pondering what Judith said about her school years, may discover that:

- Kids with disabilities are often locked away from much of the rich everyday life of their schools. And quite often, the keys to that life are on the outside. Persons with disabilities may have much to give to the spirit and the learning climate of their school, but those gifts will never be recognized and valued until so-called *regular* students cooperate with them in unlocking the doors.
- Regular students can go through all the grades without having one person with a disability as a close friend or classmate.

Human-service workers, after pondering what Judith experienced with service agencies, may realize that:

- We can become so preoccupied with developing, say, the Complete Areawide Drinking- Fountain System that we are paralyzed when one person dying of thirst suddenly comes to us for a single cup of water. After the poor guy dies, we say, "What a pity. If only our service plan had been operating in time."
- Most of us write programs that are perfect—on paper. They are like the

football plays sports announcers draw for us during televised games. Every player has an assignment, and if each one does his part, the play ends with a touchdown. The only trouble is that most plays don't end with a score. Most touchdowns probably are made by team members who, after screwing up, have the guts to get up off the ground and quickly try something else. Anything else! Judith Snow's friends didn't quit when their initial plans failed.

- It is altogether possible for us to spend all our productive years working with people who have severe disabilities, and never know one of those people as a close personal friend.

All of us can understand that:

- People with disabilities will always be a minority in their own communities. And the majority that surrounds them can exert a subtle but painful tyranny over their tiny group. The majority has more people and money, and with that power, it can control the prevailing judgment on any controversial issue raised by people with disabilities. And yet a person with a disability, together with a circle of friends and some accurate, clear-cut facts and values, can generate a spirit that may overcome or change that judgment.

# 6 - It All Started in a Pig Barn

Scott Rountree and Scott Thompson

*Springfield, Ohio*—An article in the February 22, 1986, *Springfield News-Sun* congratulated the Northwestern High School wrestling team for winning its second consecutive Central Buckeye Conference championship.

It also mentioned Scott Thompson, the team's "number one fan." How he became the Northwestern Warriors' top rooter is interesting, since he doesn't even attend that school, though he does live in that school district. But since he has a disability, and since Ohio has a dual education system—one for so-called normals and another for people with developmental disabilities—Thompson must travel to a segregated school twenty miles away every day. How he became so well-known to the students at Northwestern is explained in a taped interview with his friend Scott Rountree, captain of the wrestling team:

. . . . .

I got to know Scott [Thompson] . . . oh, about six years ago. We both happened to be in 4H. He took a pig to the county fair, and I did, too. And we got thrown together. We all had duties, and he and I had to clean the barn together, and . . . well, he overwhelmed me. I'd never met a guy like that before. Most people look at him and say he's got disabilities, but he's brighter than some of the normal kids I know. He'd do anything in the world for you. I think the world of him. He's my buddy.

He started coming to my football games, and we started getting along. And, you know, I helped him out if somebody would poke fun at him. I'd tell them don't do that.

*You say some of the kids poked fun at him?*

Yeah. There are kids who . . . I guess the reason they do it, they don't understand. I remember a few kids laughing and stuff, and trying to make jokes. And I told them to quit it. He's somebody.

At first when he came to wrestling meets, the guys on the team didn't know how to react. Then after they saw me with him, you know. Now the rest of the guys on the wrestling team—even the coach—like to be around him.

*Why was it so hard at first?*

Well . . . Scott has a special look, a different look. Some people aren't used to that. So they figure they've got to stare. But the ones who get to know him, they don't do that. And there's not too many people who'll do it in front of me. [laughs]

But he knows he's got disabilities. And he has a hard time talking. He's hard to understand at first. But all the guys that know him, they understand him.

He helps me out a lot. There was a lot of pressure on me this year. When I started to lose at the end of the season, he'd always get to me and tell me it's okay, it didn't matter. Of course, when I was in the match, he'd yell his heart out for me. I could hear him. He knows the names of all of the guys [on the team], and he yelled for them, too. But when I started losing, he'd still get to my side.

In football, it was the same thing. We didn't have a very good team. And after the game he'd be standing at the door, waiting for me to come out. And when I did, he put his arm around me. And once I intercepted a pass and ran it into the end zone. And when I ran off to the side, there he was, and he had the biggest smile!

. . . . .

Thompson and Rountree continue to be close, spending much of their leisure time together at fast-food restaurants or at the movies. They go shopping, ride bikes, and play one-on-one basketball. Last summer they painted a house together. Their favorite topic for discussion: What's happening at Northwestern High, where Thompson attends as many extra-curricular activities as possible.

"Scott [Thompson] sees Northwestern as *his* school, and many of its students as *his* best friends," said his mother.

PERSKE

Tanya Heartquist and Shawntell Strully

# 7 - A Kid Helps Her Friend Learn to Walk

Today you can buy books by the bushel on ways to teach kids with severe disabilities how to do basic things:

suck from a straw
control tongue movements
communicate
hold a spoon
crawl faster
pull to a standing position
walk or operate a wheelchair
handle bathroom needs
count money
use proper manners
worship in a church, synagogue, or mosque
get a job and hold it
fight for dignity and rights
insist on more choices in life
contribute to neighborhood betterment
take control of one's own life.

You can attend numerous conventions and conferences, where the authors of such books —usually teachers and university professors—showcase their techniques and argue over which teaching method is best. No doubt about it—all this energy has transformed the field from what it was in 1950, when all its usable texts could fit neatly on a single shelf, to what it is today, with so many how-to-do-it books the whole wing of a library couldn't house them all.

Something rich, however, is missing from almost all those texts: Most fail to show how two people can sometimes come together as friends and teach each other valuable things without consulting a book at all.

. . . . .

*Louisville, Kentucky*—Jeff Strully gave me a look of pained urgency and his voice rose.

"It wasn't the teachers who taught my daughter to walk. It was her friend!" Judging from the way Strully said it, he wanted everyone in the whole world to know how Tanya Heartquist helped Shawntell Strully learn to walk. And after hearing the story from several sources, I wanted to help him tell it.

Back in 1980, when nine-year-old Tanya attended fifth grade at Lowe Elementary School, she signed up as a member of a buddy system—kids who gave up one recess each day to help in the school's special-education class. Shawntell, only six months younger than Tanya, attended that class—and the two fixed on each other like magnets.

Outgoing and vivacious Tanya appeared to be a kid who might someday fly with eagles, while Shawntell's distinctiveness came from a long string of deficiencies which professionals had stamped on her as if she were a package damaged in the mail—"severe profound mental handicap," "cerebral palsy," "visually impaired," "nonambulatory," "repetitive myoclonic seizures." Those labels stood out so vividly that nobody seemed to notice her many strengths and gifts.

After Tanya's presence in the class for only a couple of days, Shawntell singled her out, crawled directly to her, and reached for her hand.

"I took her hand," Tanya said. "Then I'd slowly help her to stand up. This happened every time she saw me." Tanya, so moved by the compelling way she was chosen as a friend, saw Shawntell immediately as a neat person to know.

"This may sound strange," Tanya said, "but I never really saw her as disabled. She was just one of the kids. Right from the start, I liked her very much."

Although Tanya never thought of herself as teaching Shawntell, they began a daily routine: Tanya entered the room. Shawntell crawled to her. Tanya took her hand and helped her to stand. Then off the two would go, struggling to walk the school halls. When Shawntell fell down, she got back up and moved on again, with Tanya's support. Just before recess ended, they went back to the classroom, where Tanya braided Shawntell's hair.

"It took two and a half years before Shawntell could walk by herself," Jeff said, "and Tanya stuck with her all that time. Even the teachers and the physical therapists—who fiddled around with her legs every now and then—admitted that it was the walks with Tanya that did the most good."

Although the teachers always developed a written individual program plan (e.g., how to drink from a cup, how to grasp a spoon, how to avoid wet pants), the plan of choice for Shawntell was *Tanya*.

"If I could have looked inside Shawntell's head," Jeff said, "I'm sure I could have heard her saying 'I want to be with Tanya and her friends. They walk fast, so I want to walk fast. I want to do everything they are doing.'

"Let me tell you what happened during the summer after their first school year together," Jeff went on, his voice becoming emotional again. "This kid Tanya calls us and asks if she can come over and play with Shawntell. Imagine that, she called us! That never happens in families like ours. *She called us!*" he repeated. "And the next thing I know, this kid is coming on weekends with her sleeping bag."

During the next four years, the friendship thrived.

- They did all kinds of teenage things—movies, rock concerts, swimming, putt-putt golf, fairs, museums, football games, birthday parties, and horseback riding (both loved horses).
- It seemed they were always eating at one home or the other. They even celebrated some holidays together.
- Shawntell didn't talk, but she developed marvelous communication skills. For example, she always greeted Tanya with warm hugs—except when they argued. Then Shawntell gave her some forceful pushes. Once, after they had had a disagreement, they just happened to meet at the shopping mall, and Shawntell gave Tanya a hard shove, right in front of everybody.
- Early in the friendship, Shawntell wet her pants as a signal of rebellion, but as the kids focused on interesting things to do, her revolt faded.

    "Her wetting her pants didn't bother me," Tanya said. "I had no problem helping her with going to the bathroom anyway."
- Once, according to Tanya, she almost gave Shawntell's mother a heart attack when she helped her friend walk down a stairway.
- In middle school, Shawntell was integrated into regular music, art, library, and physical education classes. She traveled

on field trips and found other school chums, but Tanya remained her closest friend.

- Tanya explained to Jeff and Cindy Strully that Shawntell's room—decorated with Strawberry Shortcake characters—wasn't acceptable. So with Tanya's help, the place was elaborately redecorated with "teen stuff"—posters of Bruce Springsteen, Bryan Adams, The Cars, Rick Springfield. The ambience of the place received an added enhancement with a stereo that blared rock concert tapes.

- The same thing happened with clothes. Since Shawntell used braces during the early years of their friendship, Tanya pushed for blue jeans instead of skirts. Shawntell knew which avant garde jeans she wanted, and when someone offered her another brand, she pushed them away. When clothes were held up in front of her, she developed decided gestures to show which she liked and which she didn't.

- Some articles Shawntell's father wrote about the girls' friendship appeared in national publications, and when the middle-school principal happened to read one of them, he praised Tanya to the student body in glowing terms. This bothered Tanya so much that she told him about it in a letter.

"The principal made me out to be some kind of a hero," Tanya said. "He said I had done a 'good deed.' So I wrote him and told him that he didn't pay attention to other friendships, so why did he have to make a big deal out of this one. I felt our friendship was just like all the other friendships at school. After he received my letter, he let me know he was sorry for what he had done."

. . . . .

After four years, the Strully family relocated to Colorado and the girls' friendship faded. Although Shawntell now attends integrated classes in an Arapahoe County high school and has many new friendships, none is as close as the one with Tanya, according to Jeff and Cindy.

"I have to tell you, Shawntell's life is richer because of Tanya," Jeff told us. "She was our internal monitor for teenage things. . . . . I'm changed, too. Tanya showed us something that was way before its time. What she did has really influenced my way of looking at things."

Tanya's mom saw the relationship as a healthy natural progression in Tanya's life. "I was happy to merely let it happen. . . . It was just a case of kids being kids. But I know it had a real impact on my daughter."

Tanya, now a high school sophomore, seemed puzzled at first that someone would call long-distance for an interview. Although she felt the friendship was "no big deal," she reflected on the experience:

"Shawni opened my mind. She made me accept things. She taught me patience. She increased my ability to accept all kinds of handicaps. . . . I don't know if I'll ever see her again. I hope so. But I know she loved me . . . and I loved her."

# 8 - Hang in There, Ugly Duckling

"We know a good deal about loneliness today," said psychologist Robert Weiss during a research conference on the subject in 1982. "There is persuasive evidence that there are two forms of loneliness. One form is experienced, typically, as an aching emptiness and is a response to the *absence of an attachment figure*. The other form is experienced, typically, as a feeling of marginality, of exclusion, and is a response to the *absence of a place in an accepting community*" (Weiss, p. 3). Interestingly, a person can feel marginal and lonely when others are present—even in a large crowd.

Can you imagine how it might feel to experience either type of loneliness? Or both? There's a good chance the double-whammy ache could be so painful, you might try to shove it deep down inside—refuse to talk about it, cover it up—anything to keep it from erupting like a volcano.

I know people who bluff like that. But even though they try to hide the pain, little flashes of it appear now and then.

. . . . .

In the early 1960s I worked at an institution for children and adolescents where Thanksgiving and Christmas were the grimmest days of all. As many staff members as possible were given those days off. The wisdom of the time rated the welfare of service workers higher than that of the servees—those young people who had been labeled so indelibly they could have worn badges that said "mental retardation," "cerebral palsy," "autism," "epilepsy," "quadriplegia," "brain damage," "multiple sclerosis," and many other words that highlighted their deficiencies but ignored their strengths.

So, early on these "high days," a skeleton crew herded the residents down long hallways to a large dining hall, where the din of metal trays, the chatter, and the mingled odors of food were reminiscent of the mess-hall scene from *Oliver Twist*. Then after breakfast, the young people walked, hobbled, or wheeled to an empty-ward-turned-chapel, where they saw a short film—*The Ugly Duckling*, narrated by Jiminy Cricket (Walt Disney Productions).

Although the children had seen the film many times before, we staff members knew it would grab them again, more than any other drama. I recall how those young people leaned forward, wide-eyed and silent, each time that spunky little duckling tried to move in with the other little ducks—only to be ignored or pushed away. But he was a tough little guy. He kept coming back.

Then came the Awful Moment when a mother duck turned on the little one and shouted, "Don't you understand? You don't belong with us! Go away and stay away!" The audience froze in their seats.

This cycle repeated itself each time the little charmball encountered a group of winged youngsters, made his winsome greeting—then was shooed away by the adults. Each member of the audience was pulling for that little fellow as if he were a little brother.

Finally, after being chased away so many times, the terrible situation hit home to the little duckling. Shoulders drooping, head hanging, and tears in his eyes, he began to wander aimlessly. He felt utterly alone, ugly and unwanted.

The audience watched, mouths open. They identified body and soul with the loneliness of their little hero.

Suddenly the scene changed. A new group of young waterfowl came up to the duckling and invited him to dive in and swim with them. But he held back.

Then came the parents. And when the mother said, "You belong with us! You're a swan!" The audience *clapped*.

And when the little guy said, "Belong? A swan? You mean I'll grow up to be . . . like you?" and the adult said he would, the children *cheered*. The loneliness of the little duckling was solved—even though their own unspeakable loneliness was not.

Ruth Harper, now living in a Winnipeg, Manitoba, community of friends, remembers lonelier days.

# 9 - Fred Smith Talks About Loneliness

*Saskatoon, Saskatchewan*—Throughout the province, people with severe disabilities have begun to organize into self-advocacy groups. They support one another, try to solve problems encountered on the job and in the neighborhood, help to find their own gifts and rehearse them. But above all, they learn to speak for themselves. Many times the groups call themselves "People First" organizations— in remembrance of the woman from Salem, Oregon, who felt people with disabilities should be seen as *people first* (Perske, 1978, p. 54).

When Fred Smith, 55, joined the Outlook, Ontario, People First organization and learned to speak for himself, he recalled the loneliness caused by teasings he had received as a kid, rejection by the school district, time spent in an institution and, later, in a segregated workshop. As president of the group, he developed a remarkable way of speaking for himself and others by writing poetry. Here is one example.

WHAT ABOUT ME

When you invite someone in,
Hey! there, what about me?
Then the laughter begin;
Hey! there, what about me?

I may be in the wheel-chair,
I look for someone who's not there;
Nobody let me come in,
So my heartaches begin;

When you offer a treat to someone,
Hey! there, what about me?
When you like to have fun,
Why not with me.

You like to get along with others,
Hey! what about me;
When you like to treat one like a brother,
Hey! there, what about me.

# 10 - Carolyn Daniel Speaks Out for Her Son

*Burlington, Kentucky*—Some moms and dads fight like tigers to get their children with severe disabilities into their own neighborhood public schools, rather than have them bused to faraway segregated schools every day. And once their sons or daughters get into local schools, those parents fight just as fiercely so that their children can occupy seats in regular instead of special classes. Even then, some parents, like the writer of the following article, feel there is more to fight for:

## WANTED: JUST ONE FRIEND

How many times I have said, "If my son could make just *one* friend at school, everything would be fine!"

Of course, everything would not be fine. There will always be problems. My son is handicapped, you see. Dealing with OT, PT, IEPs, LREs and the dozen other acronyms we parents face will always be a problem. But we will deal with them, and with the help of the "experts," we will hopefully fix what can be fixed.

The social problems our children face are truly heartbreaking. We as parents (who are supposed to be able to "fix" everything) are helpless. Can and should we "buy" them friends? Can a real friend be bought?

My son has cerebral palsy, attention deficit disorder with hyperactivity, and is learning disabled. He is in the fourth grade at our neighborhood school, and the only special education he receives is an LD [learning disabled] resource room for math. He does average (or better) school work, dresses in the latest styles (demanding "hi-top" Reeboks even though velcro had meant independence), loves MTV and Garbage Pail Kids, is well liked by his teachers and office staff, and . . . doesn't have one friend at school. No one to "spend the night," eat lunch with, or even walk down the hall with.

We have tried engineering friendships with swim parties, overnights, movies, and McDonald's, only to have him waiting by the phone for that call that never comes—the invitation to their house.

This isolation takes its toll in many ways. Parents feel helpless and heartbroken. The child begins to lose interest in bringing home the good grades he is capable of. Who cares, anyway? Everyone else at school is talking about "so and so's" party last week and he wasn't invited, or worse, was invited and ignored. It causes emotionally immature LD and hyperactive adolescents to "act out" behaviors that usually result in attracting only the principal's attention. It causes a myriad of problems, but mostly a sad, lonely child.

My son is not mistreated by his classmates. On the contrary, they "mother" him. When I have expressed concern to school personnel, I've been told: "The other children love him—they help him all the time!" I hate to sound ungrateful, but helping and liking are vastly different things!

Public Law 94-142 [the U.S. government law calling for a full-service education for all children regardless of disability] gave our children the right to attend their neighborhood schools and receive an appropriate education. It has been enormously successful. But a far greater battle lies ahead—true acceptance of our handicapped children into their schools.

I sincerely wish this had a happy ending. That he had found that "best friend" we all remember from our school days. That one special friend that shared our innermost secrets, that laughed with us, cried with us, and always was there to play with us. Maybe someday my son will find that person who will see beyond his disabilities and take the time to get to know what a bright and funny little guy he really is.

If I thought it would work, I would run this ad:

WANTED: JUST ONE FRIEND.
MUST LOVE: MUSIC, DOGS, SWIMMING, BIKING, MUD, BUGS, THE FLINTSTONES, COSBY, GARFIELD AND PEANUTS SPECIALS. APPROX. 11 YEARS OF AGE. FOR LIFE.

Cynthia Jones, Monnie and Marilyn Brabham

# 11 - Seeing Cynthia Through the Eyes of the Heart

Traveling all over central Georgia with Barbara Fischer proved to be a double blessing. Barbara is a coordinator at the Macon/Bibb Citizen Advocacy Office, and she introduced me to some incredible friendships—a few of the more than three hundred she and her colleague, Frankie Lewis, have connected and nurtured during the past nine years. At the same time, this fast-paced pixie with the energy of a marathon runner exposed me to her worldview.

As we headed for a meeting with a young woman named Cynthia in the historic district of Macon, Barbara said, "I'm sure you're familiar with the story of *The Little Prince?*"

"Mmm Hmmm," I said.

"You know the passage that grabs me most?"

"Which one?"

"The one that says, 'It is only with the heart that one can see rightly.'"

"Nice statement."

"That's Cynthia. Many of us see Cynthia as magnificent. And yet, others saw her as a throwaway person. She was only twelve years old when we discovered her, and she was living in a nursing home filled with elderly people."

Barbara's philosophy made me like her all the more. But somehow—because of my lagging, more calloused view of the world—I feared the worst.

. . . . .

*Macon, Georgia*—We parked in front of two side-by-side shops, freshly painted gray with white trim, tastefully accentuated with striped awnings of the same color.

"Loving Kair Beauty Salon" was freshly painted in large white cursive letters above the awning of one shop. Over the other shop, the same kind of sign: Marilyn's Boutique. Although the outside attracted me, I expected to walk in on people who smiled tightly over gritted teeth—as if they were doing penance for past sins or trying to earn a comfortable slot in a world to follow.

I couldn't have been more wrong.

As we entered the beauty shop, I spied Cynthia in the waiting room. She sat as unmovable as concrete. Her small legs and feet contained so little muscle that the skin seemed to be stretched over bone. Her wrists and fingers looked bent and frozen. Although she was twenty years of age, she couldn't have weighed more than forty pounds.

But her face, with those large, expressive eyes—that was something else. When customers passed by, called her by name, and gave their Hellos or Good-byes, her head remained rigid, but her lovely eyes tracked them all the way in or out of the shop. Although she didn't move her jaws, she slowly flashed a wide smile.

With strangers like myself, the smile didn't come. She studied every inch of me and probably would do it for quite some time before seeing me as friend or no friend.

Barbara picked up the rigid little body, gave her a warm hug and a kiss, and we all moved through the four-chair beauty parlor. We said hello to Monnie Brabham, the owner. He told us to drop in on his wife Marilyn in the boutique next door. He would come over as soon as he had finished with the woman in his chair.

"It's really no big deal, having Cynthia with us," Marilyn said. "She's just in our family, and we love her."

The love started seven years ago when Marilyn became acquainted with Barbara, who took her to the nursing home where Cynthia lived.

"I took one look at Cynthia," said Marilyn. "Then I thought about how I'd feel if I was in an awful place like that and how much I'd hope someone would come and help me get out of there. I told Barbara I'd be Cynthia's friend."

And Marilyn did, though she and Monnie planned to exchange wedding vows within the next few days.

Marilyn picked up Cynthia at the nursing home regularly, took her out to restaurants and recreational places in the real world of Macon. She took Cynthia to her home as well. And as the two became close, Marilyn began to attack a series of unfair bureaucratic entanglements that plagued and demeaned her friend. She argued for better living conditions at the nursing home and for Cynthia's right to attend school. Later, she applied as the responsible "payee and disburser" for Cynthia's government support check. Since the funds had been misused previously, her application was quickly granted.

Finally, Marilyn concluded that Cynthia definitely did not belong in the nursing home, and with the assistance of the Macon/Bibb Citizen Advocacy office, she held a Friends of Cynthia breakfast meeting. Prominent persons in the Macon community attended, and Cynthia's need for a permanent family was presented, but no one offered to help.

Then Monnie—without any previous planning or discussion with Marilyn—stood up and announced that Cynthia was moving in with them!

Once again, the decision was made in a flash, though Marilyn was scheduled to give birth to their first child within a few days. But no matter. This couple now had a track record for making pairs of big decisions!

So Monnie IV (nicknamed Rockman) and Cynthia arrived at the same time, and the couple became a family of four.

Interestingly, Cynthia's transition involved no interviews, no papers to fill out, no lawyers, no home investigations by social workers. She just moved.

"The nursing home people said Cynthia has severe cerebral palsy and severe mental retardation, too. We disagree about the mental retardation. Maybe she can't speak, but she sees and hears everything. And she can make sounds to let you know what's going on with her. And when we scold her—oh my! How those big eyes fill with tears.

"For example, Cynthia didn't like losing some of the attention we gave Rockman," Marilyn went on. "She stopped eating—something she had never done before. Then she jumped out of her chair, falling face down on the floor. She doesn't look like she can jump, but boy, she really can. So we gave her a good talking to, and then she cried. Ever since, she and our son have been close. Then came Nicklaus, our second son, and it became even better."

When the boys come in from school, they often call out, "Where's our sister?" And when others come to take Cynthia out, the boys put them through a grilling: "Where you gonna take her? Make sure she eats well! Where's she gonna be staying? When's she gonna come home?"

Throughout our visit, I sensed that Monnie and Marilyn wondered what the big deal was—a stranger coming in like this and asking about Cynthia. Later, when I mentioned that wonderment to Marilyn over the phone, her answer came quickly:

"It isn't a big deal to us. Sure, she's some extra work, but we love her. We're just a normal family, and Cynthia is normal, too."

. . . . .

"What was it some folks used to say Cynthia was?" I asked Barbara as we drove away.

"A throwaway," Barbara said. "There are lots of people like her."

"And you can take them for the asking?"

"Sure. I know lots of them. I know the other kind, too. The kind where you usually have to go through piles of red tape—applications, interviews, investigations and all."

"Not fair, is it?"

"Nope."

Even so, ever since Monnie and Marilyn saw Cynthia with their hearts, it has been clear that no one will ever call Cynthia a throwaway kid again.

# 12 - The Thrill of Being Chosen

Suppose I live in a group home, and you are the supervisor. The government pays you to keep me, but we like each other. We even see each other as a good friend. Suppose also that both of us root blindly for the New York Yankees.

The home of good Yankee fans, our house contains all the usual memorabilia: pennants, team pictures, a poster of Dave Winfield hitting a home run, even a voodoo doll in the image of George Steinbrenner—with pins stuck in it.

Then on a sunny Saturday morning in July, you come in with two box-seat tickets for the afternoon doubleheader—the Yankees vs. the Boston Red Sox, no less. You ask me to go with you.

What a way to enjoy Saturday!

Then suppose Charlie Kindman, a neighbor who lives down the block, shows up with two bleacher tickets for the same games.

"My boss gave me the tickets," he says, "and although I'm not a great fan, I wondered if you'd like to go with me?"

Now I have a choice to make. Should I sit in a lovely box seat with you, or should I sit in a higher-up-and-farther-back seat with Charlie, a lukewarm fan. Which will I choose?

There's a good chance I would choose Charlie.

Why? Although I like you, I know you are paid to be with me. I may also be aware that all who relate to me are paid to do it or are conscripted as volunteers.

I also know that Charlie—all on his own—*chose* to take me.

. . . . .

Time passes. I take more control over my own life and, with your help, I move into an apartment and live there alone.

You, as part of a follow-up plan, drop in on me every now and then to see how I'm doing. You see me hitting it off well with some of my apartment neighbors and the shopkeepers on the street below. Some people ignore me, but that's the way it's always been. Even so, you see me slowly becoming an active participant in the life of the neighborhood.

But Charlie keeps dropping in, too. We drink beer and watch TV. We take in movies and have late-night sandwiches and pie and coffee at the diner down the street.

After a month in the apartment, Charlie asks me to go with him and some pals, Pat and Duane, on a three-day fishing trip.

The trip turns out to be a bust as far as the fishing goes, but three days of eating and laughing and feeling part of the gang . . . that's something else.

After the trip, not only does Charlie keep dropping in; Pat and Duane do, too. And those three guys launch me into the darnedest social schedule—as if I had begun to live on a different planet, with all kinds of great new things to see and do with them. Suddenly I begin to feel really alive, because of Charlie and Pat and Duane.

Three months pass. Although there are ups and downs, my friends stick with me.

Then one day you sense that I'm trying to disconnect from you. I'm too busy to talk long on the phone. I fail to keep our appointments. You may even feel I'm giving you the dodge.

I am.

Please don't take it personally. You—as skilled as you are and as great as you have been to me—represent a human-service system. I never want to be on the delivery end of a service system again if I can keep from it. I probably will choose my friends over you every time.

Would you understand?
Would you see me as an ingrate?
Would you let me go?

Kathy Marino with two members of her circle of friends—Kim Zess and Tina Dingle—at St. Mary's High School, Hamilton, Ontario

# 13 - Circles of Friends in Schools

*Toronto, Ontario*—Marsha Forest came away from her Joshua Committee experiences as if she had put on a better pair of glasses. Her position as a well-ensconced professor of special education at York University suddenly seemed less important to her. She spent long hours on the road helping school boards, principals, and teachers to see how everybody can experience richness when someone with a severe disability is placed in a regular classroom and the so-called regular students are encouraged to form a circle of friends around that person.

Forest always believed in getting teachers down to meticulous detail when it came to educating persons with disabilities. Now, however, she saw that some of the most valuable educational steps can come *naturally* from regular classmates, if the right conditions exist in the classroom. She saw how peer-group concerns can become a fountainhead of power.

She also knew that parents and teachers fear peer-group pressure. After all, when kids get together these days, they can give themselves quite an education—one that often shapes lives more powerfully than adults can shape them. But peer-group education doesn't always lead to belligerence and destruction and drugs. It can lead to caring and nurturing and helping others do healthy things they had never done before.

This twist, however, generated fears in some teachers when it dawned on them that a circle of friends might foster better growth and development in a student than they were capable of teaching.

And so Marsha moved into regular schools and worked hard at:

- helping boards and principals understand the circles-of-friends process
- finding a teacher and class willing to include a person with a severe disability
- helping the regular teacher handle any initial fears about the venture
- letting the teacher and class call the shots as much as possible
- providing strong support persons—integration facilitators—who would assist only when they really were needed
- then finding a handful of kids willing to work at being friends with their classmate with the disability.

"The first placement in a school is the toughest," she said. "After that, it's usually easy to include others."

Forest sees the building of a circle of friends as a person-by-person process, not an all-encompassing program. And so she focuses on students with disabilities one at a time, setting up a framework that enables a circle to surround that person.

Because no two settings are alike, she watches as the circle, the regular teacher, and the rest of the students develop and coordinate their own routines for helping. Then, never predicting an outcome, she waits. And when new learning takes place in the person with the disability, Forest moves in and makes all the students, the teacher, the principal—even the board members—feel simply great.

According to her, the average school can handle up to twelve of these arrangements. After that, the efficiency of the process may diminish.

She doubts that circles of friends will work in every school. "If a school is all screwed up," she said, "and if it has lost its zest and commitment for really helping kids learn— forget it. On the other hand, I'm sure that circles of friends can help make a good school —and especially the kids—better. Then coming to school takes on fresh values and meaning. Some enjoy coming to school as they never did before."

According to Forest . . .

"Circles of friends are not an alternative to learning. They are a precondition.

"They move us beyond integration—into community.

"I hate labels. I just see people who challenge the school system.

"Wait for schools to be ready for people with challenging behaviors, and you can wait until hell freezes over.

"The term *gifted* is an insult. All people have gifts. Sometimes those with challenging behaviors have the greatest gifts.

"You can't learn to like kids with disabilities by watching puppets. Puppets don't smell or drool. They aren't real. Kids learn to accept people with differences by really living with them."

# 14 - Keep Carla from Being Mowed Down

School chums Amanda Woehrle and Carla Barbadoro

*Hamilton, Ontario*—Carla Barbadoro, her head barely clearing her desk, appears to be among giants in the seventh- and eighth-grade class at St. Agnes Elementary School. But she is age twelve, like many of her classmates. And although her developmental disabilities have kept her looking and functioning like a first-grader, everyone agrees that she is better off in a class with kids her own age than in a special one.

Carla had attended the school since kindergarten, but she was always in classes with younger students. Then a year ago, it was decided to place her with kids her own age. So she was just moved in. No special-education support persons appeared for two weeks. That way, regular teacher Peter Mamer and his students got to know Carla on their own, and *they* decided what her educational plan should contain.

Interestingly, they learned right away that when Carla walked out the door into the hall, other kids—not seeing her because of her size—knocked her flat. So without waiting for anyone's approval, they moved quickly to Goal 1: Look out for Carla in crowds.

Although she has a circle of eight close friends who help her with her studies, every student helps with Goal 1, serving as a shield for Carla.

When some of the students were asked if Carla really belonged in the class, big burly Dino Borchetta, who sits next to her, responded quickly: "I don't care how disabled a kid is. If she isn't with kids her own age, she's lost."

But what about the difference in the studies?

"When you are good at seventh-grade stuff," said Melita Frketic, "it's easy to help her with first-grade reading." Consequently, the students exhibit confidence and pride as they help Carla with her schoolwork. Quite frankly, Carla seems more ready to learn from her peers than from her teacher.

Also, Carla receives numerous informal educational opportunities offered by her classmates, which never could be offered in a special-education class. For example, during recess, a group of girls liked to sing the songs they'd learned at camp the previous summer, and they invited Carla to join the group. Today she can sing all the songs and do the hand motions, too.

Carla has learned to flirt with Dino, a skill that fails to appear in her regular curriculum. And yet Carla knows how to look up into the big guy's face and seductively roll her eyes. Obviously, she has been watching other girls in the class. Students don't receive grades for such things, but her achievement appears to rate an easy A+.

# 15 - Larry, As His Friends See Him

*Hamilton, Ontario*—Sixteen-year-old Larry O'Brien's friends at St. Marys' High School had just finished getting to know him when I visited their room. They had taped large sheets of paper on the wall, and many student-inspired ideas had been written on them with a magic marker:

## WHAT ARE YOUR DREAMS FOR LARRY?

— to have a social life
— to have a meaningful job he is happy doing
— to share a house or apartment with others his own age
— to have friends

## WHAT COULD BE LARRY'S NIGHTMARES?

— no real friends
— no meaningful job
— to live with paid staff or in an institution

## WHO IS LARRY?

— friendly
— charming
— aggressive
— romantic
— cheerful
— generous
— fun
— frustrated
— stubborn
— nonverbal
— grabby

## LARRY'S NEEDS

— to learn to behave properly in the cafeteria
— to not grab people and things
— to get off the bus properly
— to communicate effectively
— to sit still and listen
— more guys
— to learn to match numbers
— to learn to count
— to be part of classes (gym, English, typing, art, math, drama, computers)

## POSSIBLE JOBS

| In the Community | In School |
|---|---|
| — mailman | — cut grass |
| — bag boy in grocery | — put cards in library books |
| — garbageman | |
| — take tickets at movie theater | — coat room at school dances |
| — coat check man | — pick up paper on school grounds |
| — bellboy at hotel | |
| — put food trays on wagon in hospital | — work with janitor clean sweep |
| — snack bar | — in cafeteria put food out clean tables |
| — packaging/ unpacking | |
| — work with younger children | — in office deliver messages staple papers put mail in slot |
| — work at nursing home | — fill pop machines |

The students participate in regular planning sessions to produce charts on Larry's behalf. According to faculty members at St. Mary's, each session becomes more sophisticated, focused and relevant to Larry, the friend the students are getting to know better and better.

Katherine Woronko and one of her circle of friends, Rita Lipani

# 16 - Uniform No. 3 Remains in Its Box

*Richmond Hill, Ontario*—Fourteen-year-old Katherine Woronko couldn't speak. She lived in a world of her own, where she stared into space, twiddled objects before her eyes, tried to put everything in her mouth, and whined for no apparent reason. She had been diagnosed as having profound retardation.

"Katherine attended a school for 'the trainable retarded,'" said her father, Stan Woronko. "There and at home, we worked on behavior modification programs. But her only contacts were her family and the specialists at the school. So we burned out on the programs and became dissatisfied with the school. But we never even imagined what it would be like for Katherine if she had friends."

Then came the opportunity to enroll Katherine in St. Robert High School as a ninth grader. Preparing for the worst, Stan and his wife, Marthe, purchased three complete school uniforms. And they wondered whether they should have bought four. The third uniform has never been out of the box.

Today Katherine is in the eleventh grade. She begins her morning with a twenty-minute aerobic workout and a half hour of weight lifting in the nautilus room. She has a home room, attends regular academic classes as well as band and dramatic arts, and is learning work skills in the library. She even goes to the school dances. Although she can't speak, she knows some hand signs and can signal her own responses and needs. Today a visitor at St. Robert, seeing the now prim and proper Katherine in the halls, would never believe this was the same student who entered the school two years ago.

Katherine's first days at school were rough for everyone. Fortunately, integration facilitator Annmarie Ruttimann stayed at her side throughout each school day. Ruttimann—who does not believe in asking for volunteers—found other ways to involve some of the students and guided them into becoming a caring and enthusiastic part of Katherine's circle. They met regularly to discuss their own activities with Katherine and to decide on the best educational plans for her.

Today, the students—not Ruttimann—carry out a schedule of support and guidance for Katherine, from the moment she leaves her house until she returns home. The schedule is precise. The kids even serve as backups if unforeseen things happen. For example, in February of Katherine's first year, Ruttimann became ill and was away from school for a month.

"I thought everything would collapse because there was no one to take her place," Mr. Woronko said. "But it didn't. The students took responsibility for everything. That shows what kids can do when they are committed to someone like Katherine."

Katherine, of course, doesn't even begin to achieve the standards set for regular students, but she learns many things she never would learn outside the class. And since she always has a friend with her, class disruptions are rare.

Many students outside her circle have become more tolerant because of her presence. Just by watching the other students, they have come to understand Katherine. They greet her regularly and see her as a student-in-full-standing.

And Katherine has gained some interesting skills:

- *Gum Chewing.* Often, to the annoyance of everyone, Katherine walked down the hall grinding her teeth. Then one girl, thinking gum chewing was the trendy thing to do, took Katherine aside and put a stick of gum in her mouth. Then, guiding Katherine's jaws with her hands, showed her how to chew and enjoy it without swallowing it. Now, thanks to the gum, teeth grinding rarely occurs.
- *Quietness in Class.* When Katherine made noises in class, one friend learned to touch her Adam's apple and apply a slight amount of pressure. When the noises ceased, the friend passed the story of

her success to the rest of Katherine's friends.

- *Climbing Steps.* At first Katherine put her feet together on each step. Then a friend stood behind her and softly pushed on the back of a knee until she learned to put her feet on alternate steps. This skill also was shared with the rest of the circle.
- *Trendy Clothes.* "We always tried to get the same kind of clothes that Katherine's classmates wore," Mr. Woronko said. "And Katherine's friends helped us make Katherine 'trendy.' They went shopping with us. They even gave Katherine hairdos and put makeup on her. Makeup was something we hadn't even thought about." Today Katherine does indeed look trendy. She wears sweaters and T-shirts a couple of sizes too large, just as the others do. The friends even convinced the Woronkos never to let Katherine wear a uniform right from the store. "They reminded us to shorten and tighten the skirt so she would look like the other kids," said Mr. Woronko.
- *Responding to Straight Talk.* Teenage friends have a no-nonsense way of dealing with one another, and Katherine isn't exempt. "C'mon, Katherine, knock it off" or "Hey, Katherine, quit dragging behind" or "Stand up straight" or "Aw, Katherine, that's weird" are candid responses from the other students. And even though she cannot totally dress herself, the friends have shown her how to do some things.

When one teacher walked into the locker room and spied Katherine getting dressed, she said, "Ohhhh Kathy! Look at Yooou! You're dressing yourself! Gooood girl!" Behind the teacher, some of the teenagers grabbed their throats and faked retches.

According to the Woronkos, Katherine's home life has been enriched, too. Friends show up at the house uninvited. At other times, they are invited over for chili or pizza parties. The house has become a headquarters for regular and emergency circle meetings. Mrs. Woronko, so moved by all that has happened, attended a meeting at the school and thanked them for including Katherine: "For the first time we and Katherine have a sense of belonging. She has a real school to belong to. She even went to a regular dance without her parents. She's not a *case* anymore. Now she's a person who is a student, who has friends, and she goes to different classes like a real teenager."

# 17 - Can Friendships Help Revolutionize Schools?

On August 24, 1974, *Saturday Review World* celebrated its fiftieth anniversary, and editor Norman Cousins asked leading thinkers to contribute articles that would peer fifty years into the future—to the year A.D. 2024. Each was asked to predict how the human mind and spirit will respond to the hard challenges faced in his or her own field. The outcome: a rich feast of ideas from thoughtful people—Dubos, Sakharov, Bundy, Asimov, Hesburgh, Cousteau, DeBakey, and many more. Of all the back issues of the magazine, I think this one stands at the top of the list.

Harold Howe II, former U.S. Commissioner of Education, then president for Education and Research of the Ford Foundation, wrote about the status of schools. The title of his article, "Report to the President of the United States from the Chairman of the White House Conference on Education, August 1, 2024," served as a nice device for grabbing and holding readers.

According to Howe, the young people of 2024 will be soured by simply competing for the highest marks in the class, vaunted scholarships, and other top-of-the-heap honors so prevalent in today's schools. They will see the heavy emphasis on *competitive* education as destructive and will argue for *cooperative* values and practices in schools and colleges.

The report's keynote:

The student who is proficient at reading or mathematics or who does accurate and high-quality work in the sciences is not necessarily rewarded. The assumption is that he has done well because his particular combination of heredity and environment made that achievement possible. He deserves no recognition for measuring up to his potential.

What the schools and colleges increasingly reward is not the student's own achievement but his contribution to the achievement of others. And the higher his own attainments in learning, the more he is expected to do in helping others to learn.

Students with disabilities and so-called regular students who have enriched one another's lives will say, "Of course that's right. Why don't more people see it that way?"

But Howe says some won't. In fact, he predicts that 50 percent of the schools will favor this viewpoint, and 50 percent will not. And those who oppose the new direction will be organized and ready to battle for its death. He names the resisting factions:

— *Traditionalists*, who will see competition as the basis for academic excellence and character development.
— *Organized teachers and professors*, who will refuse to change their roles or modify their present job security.
— *Teacher trainers*, who will see that a cooperative approach in education will make their methods obsolete.
— *The athletic lobby* made up of people committed to the spectator and profit-making aspects of athletics—people who refuse to recognize sports as something all students should be doing for fun.

Will the intangible forces generated in friendships between so-called regular students and those with disabilities help tilt education toward healthy cooperation?

Jeremy Estep and his friends

# 18 - Kids Adjust to One Another's Life-styles, and Learning Is Enriched Too

*Louisville, Kentucky*—After watching the ballgame between Jeremy Estep and his friends, one could see that nobody treats him as handicapped. The wheelchair is almost ignored, and Jeremy gives and takes with the others so vigorously, he doesn't feel he has a handicap—just a different life-style. Friendships like this one abound at Hawthorne Elementary School, where 65 of the 350 students have disabilities.

And according to principal Patricia Lambert, as students transfer from special to regular classes, the friendships—and the education—become better for everyone.

Educational researcher Wynn DeBevoise echoed this fact when her son Lyn began attending Hawthorne. The researcher described what happened in the March 1986 issue of *Principal,* a national magazine for elementary school administrators:

In a casual conversation with a friend, I was told, "Hawthorne is a school that caters to the handicapped." This person . . . suggested that Lyn, who had been in gifted programs before coming to Louisville, would suffer academically from being placed in a school with a high percentage of handicapped students. I must admit I began to feel uneasy.

My uneasiness was short-lived, however, as I became increasingly aware that for Lyn, being in a school where handicapped children were integrated into classes and activities as fully as possible was providing positive educational experiences he would not have received from any curriculum designed for the gifted.

DeBevoise, on the basis of interviews and classroom observations at Hawthorne, concluded that everyone is enriched by the setting—students, parents, teachers, and support staff. Two highlights of many from her article:

Last year one buddy took his responsibility for helping his partner with the handicap, Freddy, a little too seriously. In the cafeteria line, he picked up the catsup bottle and poured a generous amount on Freddy's plate. Freddy, feeling he had an equally serious responsibility for his buddy, reciprocated by doling out a blob of catsup on his plate. When Freddy's buddy asked, "What are you doing?" Freddy replied, "I'm taking care of you the way you took care of me."

"A visitor got caught in a fire drill one day when I was helping out [said Cindy Williams, mother of a fifth-grader]. While we were waiting outside, she asked, 'Why are there so many handicapped students here?' My mind went blank for a second, then I found myself saying, 'We're just lucky, I guess.' "

Co-op renters Catherine Schaefer, David Wright, and Darlene Braun

# 19 - The Joy of Living in a Co-op House with Catherine

Remember writer/cartoonist James Thurber, who believed houses had personalities? In many of his cartoons he made the front facades of houses look like large faces, with eyes, a nose, and a mouth—each exuding its own distinctive mood. In some of his drawings, a man could be seen walking up to a house that smiled down on him—or one with angry eyes and a mouth ready to snarl.

I found a house that seemed to have a human face. If Thurber had drawn this one, the face would have been laughing with unabashed joy.

*Winnipeg, Manitoba*—The renters who live in the old white three-story house that has been divided into apartments at 822 Preston seem to laugh a lot. Of course they hurt and feel sad, too. But for some reason, visiting friends—who always seem to be coming and going—recall the happy times more than the sad ones. Some outsiders are so impressed with the atmosphere of the place, that they wait for an apartment to be vacated so they can try for it.

Catherine Schaefer serves as the heart of the house. And yet, twenty-seven years' worth of professional opinions usually tilted toward the notion that she could be a center only for anguish and pain. Maybe that's one of the reasons everyone laughs so much.

Actually, the flouting of professional opinion began in 1961, when Catherine was born with brain damage so severe it was said she'd never walk or talk or feed herself. Almost from the start, human service workers advised Ted and Nicola Schaefer to institutionalize their child. They refused. Later, when younger brothers Dominic and Benjy joined the family, they developed the same fierce loyalty. Consequently, Catherine became a positive force not only in their family but in their hometown as well.

In 1978, Nicola, with the directness of Walter Lippmann and the humor of Erma Bombeck, wrote *Does She Know She's There?* exposing to the world what went on in the Schaefer household. The book became a best seller, but more important, it helped other families with children having disabilities to hope and laugh and listen to their own hearts, as they may not have done before.

And yet, being a former human-service worker myself, I recall some of my colleagues saying a few years ago, in a we-love-kittens-but-we-don't-like-cats tone, "Okay. But just wait until that kid becomes an adult."

That time has come. Today Catherine, age twenty-seven, has moved away from home and lives on Preston Street with several nondisabled renters who are connected to her as caring friends:

- Darlene Braun, Catherine's apartment mate and at-home assistant
- The MacLellens—Lauchie, a nurse at the local hospital; Evelyn, a Montessori teacher; and four-year-old Marie
- Colleen Nordstrom, a financial manager in a business office
- Leanne Dyck, a university undergraduate
- David Wright, a former corporation executive who became interested in people with disabilities.

Joanne Zborowsky, a graduate student, isn't a renter, but she sometimes stays with Catherine on weekends when Darlene is away.

The house is set up as a co-op by Prairie Housing Cooperative, Inc., an organization that includes a few people with disabilities in housing situations with others who are non-disabled. Basically, the rent pays for the house. Catherine, because of her disability, does receive support from the government—but less than half what it would cost to keep her in an institution.

There is, however, one loosely stated condition for living in Prairie Housing Co-op that is discussed before members move in: All members in each residence are asked to be informal friends of the person with the disability. That's all. No set rules. How and when they connect is up to them. Does it work? The friends who live with Catherine think so.

"They pay well at the hospital," said Lauchie, "but I have this other satisfaction, coming home and doing something for Catherine every now and then—doing something that's freely given."

"We love it here," said Evelyn. "We are people who are interested in good, basic living—we're not merely interested in making money and getting ahead." Little Marie showed her feelings by wanting to sit next to Catherine when I took a picture of the group.

Colleen said she liked playing with money during the day, but "I'm so much happier now that I'm connected to the people in this house, too."

Leanne spoke of being away from her family for the first time, and how good it felt to be in *this* family.

But what about Catherine?

- *On Being Catherine's Friend:* "I was reluctant to talk," said Darlene when asked about her speech before the Canadian Association for Community Living. "When I got up there, I told them I thought it was silly to even talk about it. It was just so natural, being somebody's friend. But I talked about Catherine and me going out with people and being with people . . . about how she annoys me at times—like when she grinds her teeth—and how I get on her nerves and we straighten things out. She really is my friend. She knows more about me than anybody else. [laughs] Gee! If Catherine ever speaks, the stories she could tell! [more laughter]"
- *On Whether Catherine Knows She's There:* "She knows everything that goes on," said Darlene. "She just has her own way of communicating, and I don't see that as her disability—it's mine. I have to learn her language. She understands English perfectly . . . For the last few months, I've been going through a lot of different things in my life. And Cath rubs my face or takes my hand and squeezes it. . . . She gives, too."
- *On Choosing Friends:* "If Cath doesn't like someone, she'll let you know," said Darlene. "She will totally ignore you—evade eye contact, look around the room, put her head down. If you come too close, she'll even push you away. . . . Or she can begin laughing because she's so happy to see you."
- *On Mother-Friend Differences:* Although Nicola is a superconscientious mom, Darlene can get different responses from

Catherine. Darlene works hard to let Catherine make her own choices—something mothers might not always do. It is now clear that when it comes to clothes, Catherine likes soft colors—pinks and light greens. Nicola likes bright colors. When the apartment was being set up, Nicola intended to just go out and get the furniture . . . until Darlene reminded her that since Catherine would be using it, she should be allowed to choose. Nicola senses a strong bonding between Catherine and Darlene, and she understands and supports it.

- *On Entertainment:* "We go everywhere," said Darlene. "Lots of friends drop by to go out with her, too. We go dancing where people aren't worried about the wheelchair. Leanne went with her to a school play. We saw *Crocodile Dundee*—which she loved—and *Witches of Eastwick*—which I loved and she hated. We even go out to four-course dinners."

"Don't forget about the male strippers," Leanne added. She and Darlene looked furtively at Nicola and laughed.

Nicola laughed, too. "I'd never have gone with her," she said, "but three of her friends did a couple of years ago, and Cath thought it was wonderful. Giggled all the way through, and nonstop for several days afterward."

- *On Support from Other Members of the House:* "It's really neat," Darlene said. "We never lock our doors. If I have to leave for a while, I can open my door and let the rest know, and I know everything will be okay. Also because there's always somebody in the house, no crook would ever try to get away with something."

During the day I spent at their house, every renter made me welcome. I watched Darlene's concern for Leanne, who was coming down with a cold. I saw her work confidently with Catherine, who suddenly choked on a cracker.

She joined with others to borrow some of Lauchie's tools to get a flat tire off Catherine's wheelchair and hustled to various shops until she found one that would fit. Then she fixed a meal for Catherine, Leanne, Colleen, and me.

At dinner, Catherine, who swiped a glance at me every now and then but still refused to make eye contact, let me know her jury was still out on whether to accept me.

At the end of the evening, everyone in the house gathered and talked about their life together (for my benefit). They saw great humor in a government licensing man who came with his clipboard to see if Catherine was being cared for properly. Seemingly unable to sense the richness of the personal interactions in the house, he wrote them up for a lack of draperies in the kitchen.

As people began to sum up their experience, Joanne touched on something they all seemed to feel: "Catherine laughs at me a lot. She makes me feel warm"—laughter is her litmus test for accepting one as a friend.

Just before the meeting ended, Nicola spoke softly: "I'm profoundly grateful that my daughter has such incredible friends."

. . . . .

"What a great household," I said to Nicola as we drove away.

"It is, isn't it," she replied. "And what makes it great is that so many beautiful, ordinary things happen there. For instance, did you notice what Darlene and Leanne and Cath were wearing?"

"Well, not really. I mean, they all looked good."

"I know, but the interesting, unspectacular thing is that those pretty earrings Leanne was wearing belong to Darlene. Cath's shirt is Leanne's, and Darlene's pants belong to Catherine. In other words, it's all just like any other three young women who share an apartment."

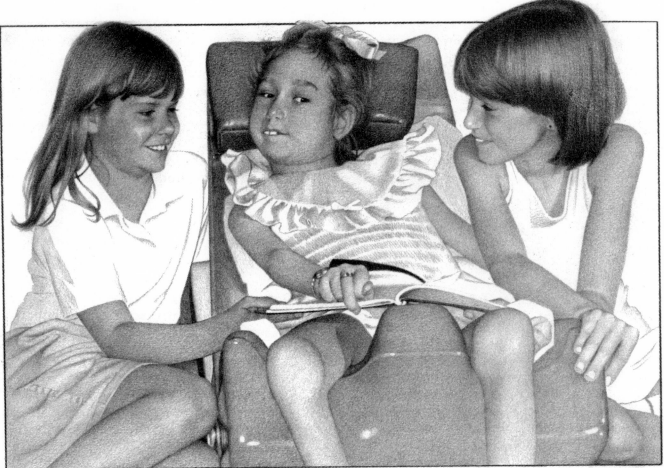

Cassi Carpenter, Ashley Lanier, and Patricia Taylor

# 20 - Kids Need Friends Their Own Age

*Richmond Hill, Ontario*—So spoke a student during a round-the-circle interview at St. Robert High School: "Folks think that when kids get together with others their own age, they only learn bad things. That's not so. There's lots of good things we teach each other. And we teach them better than anybody else. As a matter of fact, I don't care how disabled a kid is, that kid is bad off without a friend his [or her] own age."

*Savannah, Georgia*—Although Ashley Lanier cannot speak and has severe physical disabilities, she has been able to establish and maintain a friendship of exceptional quality with her good friend Cassi Carpenter. Using nods, smiles, touches, eye contact, and lots of sixth sense, the girls busy themselves with all kinds of activities—games, videos, music. They make greeting cards and send them to friends. On other days, Ashley likes Cassi to read to her or blow soap bubbles around her. But most of all, Ashley loves to watch her friend dress a favorite doll, Corinne, and fix her hair.

These two ten-year-olds have been getting together at least once a week for more than a year. On some days, Cassi brings friends with her—friends like Patricia Taylor.

Ashley's parents, Allen and Peggy, commented, "Raising a child with a profound disability is a monumental challenge. The issue can be complex and often without resolve. There are, however, aspects of life which are common to all children—the common need for love, self-worth, and friendship with other children."

"All the kids in the neighborhood know and respect Ashley," Peggy said, "but most of the girls are younger. So Cassi makes it possible for her to have a friend her own age. That really helps."

"The friendship between Ashley and Cassi really took off," said Chatham-Savannah Citizen Advocacy coordinator Tom Kohler, who introduced the youngsters. "Nobody could have predicted that Cassi and Ashley would connect as well as they do. But that's the neat thing about getting people together. It's the mystery. The unknowns. You can never predict the outcome. But I know one thing now. Both Ashley and Cassi are gaining values that can shape their lives—things that kids seldom learn in formal school lessons."

Catcher Spencer Hutchings and
batter Justin Fandl of Westchester County,
New York

PERSKE

# 21 - Special Friends?

LONELY?

NEED A FRIEND?

CALL SPECIAL FRIENDS

CALL NOW: 333-7143

So said the cover of a brochure created by a human-services agency that must recently have discovered a large empty space in the lives of the people it served.

Inside the brochure, the reader learns that Special Friends matches ordinary citizens to people with disabilities in three phases: Intake (an initial meeting with the Special Friends coordinator); Orientation (three Thursday-evening sessions); and Matching Night (a wine-and-cheese party). The back of the brochure contains another message: A SPECIAL FRIEND IS WAITING FOR YOUR CALL.

Mark Twain once said that any time you can get your hands on a modifier, you should kill it. Maybe the time has come to go after the adjective *special* every time it is used to describe people with disabilities:

— special education
— special educators
— special classrooms
— special recreation
— special buses
— special religion classes
— the matinee for special
  people
— now special friends,
  and on and on it goes.

When you hear *special* used this way, grab it by the throat and do it in!

Feeling special might be heartwarming if one is ensconced in a milieu of human beings where everybody is forced to look alike, act alike, and live according to common denominator rules—like privates in a large army, or oarsmen on a Viking ship, or kids drowning in an overcrowded ghetto—youngsters so hungry to be seen as special that they leave their own graffiti signatures wherever they can.

Being seen as special might not be so bad, either, if you're a top celebrity or the national champion of something, since it might bring lots of strokes and perks—and banks full of money.

But if you've been . . .

— singled out as not . . . normal
— given a label (it used to be an unpardonable sin for anyone "not normal" to run around without a label)
— excluded from full presence and participation in one's own neighborhood
— existing in an off-to-the-side residence
— putting in time in artificial, out of the real world programs

. . . if you felt you wanted to live "in the middle of things" in your neighborhood, but everyone saw to it that you lived only on the margins, calling you *special* might only add to the wound you already feel.

. . . . .

"Robert, this is Miss Hypotenuse calling. I'm the coordinator of the Special Friends program. I have some good news."

"You have?"

"Yes. A man called in who's looking for a special friend, and I thought of you."

"Thank you, Miss Hypotenuse, but I'm not interested."

"Robert, how can you say that?"

"Easily. Please call me when someone is interested in a *regular* friend. Okay?"

Clarence Asham and Ziggy Brazauskas

# 22 - Clarence's Gift, and the Friend Who Helped Him Rehearse It

In the middle 1700s, Thomas Gray sat down in a graveyard and wrote about the people under the stones whose talents had remained unrecognized and unrealized.

Today, some believe that *all* of us are born with certain gifts. And we need others to sense them, to help us develop them and make them flower. If that's true, "Elegy Written in a Country Churchyard" should haunt us all.

. . . . .

*Portage, Manitoba*—Twenty-five years ago, psychiatric nurse Zigmus "Ziggy" Brazauskas worked at the twelve-hundred bed Manitoba School for Retardates (now known as Manitoba Developmental Center), carrying out all the common-denominator duties one must do to manage fifty young boys on a single ward. But one boy, Clarence Asham, admitted in 1959 at age six, grabbed Ziggy's attention more each year. Although Clarence was blind and psychologists said he had an IQ of only 34, Ziggy noticed that the youngster liked to tap on things with a spoon—on the walls, the radiators, the table, anything that would make a noise—as if he were searching for a certain sound. And he would sit by the radio for hours, listening to music.

Ziggy had played the violin, mandolin, and accordion in Lithuania before World War II. He watched this tapping with increasing interest and, when Clarence was eleven, Ziggy tried some experiments. He played a note on a piano and watched Clarence tap the piano keys until he found the same note.

Then Ziggy began to take Clarence to his home after work.

"I got him acquainted with the accordion," Ziggy said. "He loved the sounds it made. So pretty soon I was taking him home four or five nights a week. There was no program like this at the institution, so I had to do it during my 'off' hours. . . . I had to do it as his friend."

For a month, Clarence was helped to make sense out of the accordion's buttons and keyboard. "It was hard work—really hard work," Ziggy said.

Then one day Clarence played his first tune, "Over the Waves."

"Once he had it, he had it *good*," Ziggy said. "After that, he loved playing so much—and so did I—that he came home with me on weekends, and we played together from 8:00 in the morning until 10:00 or 11:00 at night."

And so for many years, both did their time at the institution—one as an employee and the other as an inmate—while they looked forward to their time off together.

Ziggy also became Clarence's special protector at the institution. For example, some staff members saw Clarence as aggressive and suggested medication.

"I fought it," Ziggy said. "After all, if someone took my radio, I'd punch the guy in the nose, too."

Through the years, Clarence's musical skill soared, surpassing that of his teacher. He could play a tune from start to finish after hearing it only once. He became proficient on the accordion and also learned to play the piano, guitar, and harmonica.

By the time Clarence was fifteen, he and Ziggy had become a well-known accordion duo. From 1966 through 1968, they made 150 appearances across Canada, including the Canadian Broadcasting Corporation's "National," "Journal," and "24 Hours" programs.

"When we started traveling, I saw terrific changes in Clarence," Ziggy said. "After a five-day tour in Toronto, he came back speaking full sentences!" Clarence usually had responded by merely saying "yes" or "no."
"After all, people listened to him and talked to him in Toronto. At the institution, people didn't really talk to him that much."

Today Clarence lives in Winnipeg, in a home he shares with Ranall Ingalls, a seminary student, and Lilian Doig, a woman who had raised her own family and learned about Clarence through the pastor of her church.

When you enter their home during the day, you walk into a house filled with music, one popular or classical piece after another. Clarence can play anything! He's so good at it, his friends try to stump him with obscure requests. As for his IQ . . . well, folks don't really know anymore. But they are sure it isn't 34!

More important, Clarence, now thirty-five, is beautifully connected to his community. He takes formal music lessons at the University of Manitoba, and he and Ranall are members of St. John's College Singers, a voluntary choir group. With Lilian, he attends every production of the Winnipeg Symphony Orchestra, the Winnipeg Opera Association, and the Manitoba Chamber Orchestra—then he goes home and plays every note he heard.

"He has really discovered people," Ranall said. "Now he's aggressive about going to the door when someone rings the bell. He wants to talk about everything that's happening. That's a long way from just saying 'no' and 'yes.'"

"Clarence is a nice man—a really nice man," said Lilian. "It's a privilege to live in the same house with him and hear all his music."

"Ziggy is still Clarence's best friend," Ranall said. "You ask him, and he'll tell you."

Before Ziggy retired in 1982, some bouts of surgery forced him to give up music. Now, however, he's regaining strength, and he drops in on Clarence regularly.

I witnessed one such occasion. Clarence was at the piano, playing a piece from Rachmaninoff when Ziggy came in the front door. He walked up to Clarence quietly and touched his shoulder.

"Ziggy!" Clarence shouted. Then he laughed with joy.

The two talk about doing their act again. Maybe they will.

# 23 - Now the Telephone Rings for Them

*Wolfeboro, New Hampshire*—Dave and Merrill Rich have always enjoyed gettogethers with warmhearted friends. So they helped Becky, their ten-year-old daughter, enjoy the same kind of gatherings by inviting kids her age to come over and play, even though Becky had been set apart from the "regulars" in school because she had a Down Syndrome label and attended a special-education class.

The Riches saw to it that the kids Becky invited had a good time—so much so that when they left, they usually said they would call to invite Becky to their houses.

So Becky waited for the phone to ring for her.

But it never did.

"We saw Becky crumbling before our eyes," Dave said. "She'd light up when the promises were made. And each time they weren't kept, her self-image was destroyed just a little more."

Finally Becky's parents dreamed up a scheme. Without her knowledge, they sent letters to eight families with ten-year-old kids whom Becky liked. The letter explained the situation to the families and asked for their help:

It would mean having Becky over to your house about once every six or eight weeks, after school for one or two hours, to play with [the child's name]. We will call you to arrange a convenient afternoon for parent and daughter to invite Becky over. *Then you daughter will call Becky* [author's emphasis] at 569-4524 to invite her over for the afternoon after school. Becky will go home with your daughter, and we will pick her up between 4:30 and 5:00 P.M.

Seven of the eight families accepted the offer. The Riches then invited the families to their home, where they discussed parent and child concerns, Becky's condition, and how to best deal with her needs.

"Becky had one of the best years of her life," Dave said. "When the phone began to ring for her—with kids saying, 'please come over to my house'—her self-image soared."

Three years have passed. Although all Becky's successes may not be attributed to her parents' telephone scheme, Becky is now a full-fledged member of a "regular" Girl Scout troop, plays on an intramural basketball team, and has been largely integrated into a regular class at school, with supportive teachers to help her achieve success.

. . . . .

*Many Towns, Ontario*—In schools where circles of friends work at getting to know their newfound friends with disabilities, "telephone trees" have developed. Each circle member signs up on a telephone schedule. Then each friend with a disability receives a telephone call every night.

Al Cissell, his mother Irene, and Alice Smith

# 24 - Friends Keep a Family from Being Pulled Apart

*Macon, Georgia*—Except for a number of medicine bottles on the dining-room table, the first-floor apartment was homey and neat. And when silver-haired Irene Cissell came from one of the bedrooms, she looked pale, tired, and thin in her housecoat. But she smiled and insisted on sitting at the table. Her friend Alice Smith—a warm, gentle woman, her tone expressing love and support—sat beside her and made sure she was comfortable.

Irene spoke in a whisper: "These months have been tough. But I'm coming back."

Those who know Irene agree. She is coming back. But there wouldn't have been much for her to come back to if it hadn't been for three friends—and two citizen advocacy coordinators who got them all together.

Two years earlier, Irene had lived in a housing project with her grown children, Al and Becky. All three had been labeled mentally retarded and received support from a human-service agency. When Irene went into the hospital for major surgery, the agency placed her son and daughter in temporary homes elsewhere in town.

After the surgery, the agency thought Irene should go to a nursing home and the children should be placed in separate group homes. That is, if they could find openings. If not, Al and Becky would be sent to Central State Hospital, an institution in Milledgeville, thirty-five miles away.

Earlier, Macon/Bibb Citizen Advocacy had found advocates for Al and Becky, so when the agency planned to split the Cissell family, those advocates, Jim Brenner and Debbie Helmer, called the advocacy office. At that point, Barbara Fischer and Frankie Lewis, advocacy coordinators who enter such crisis situations, moved quickly to find an advocate for Irene. And Frankie found Alice Smith, a retired hospital communications clerk.

Irene, feeling helpless about what the agency was doing, asked Alice to go with her to the agency team meetings that focused on her family problem, so Alice and Debbie Helmer attended several of those meetings.

Alice said, "The staff members were adamant about separating them. So I asked why. One said it was the best thing to do. She said Irene waited on them all the time . . . and she'd be doing lots of things she wasn't supposed to be doing. Well, I told them I'm a mother, too, and I understood why Irene didn't want to lose her family."

Finally, the agency, moved by the concern of Alice and Debbie and Jim, decided to look for an alternative. So the three, still exerting pressure as only concerned friends can do, joined the workers in managing some remarkable changes:

- Alice became coordinator of the family's meager funds from Social Security.
- Alice and the other friends helped the family get out of the housing project and rent an apartment in West Macon.
- The Cissells were helped to get on a food stamp program.
- The agency provided a staff person who comes in to help with cleaning, cooking, and general upkeep of the apartment.
- Alice drops in on the family every day, and like a caring relative, she does the numerous things that keep the home the stability zone it was meant to be. She figures the bills, checks the medicines, helps with shopping, and takes Irene out for drives and dinners at restaurants.

Although the energies the friends have expended can never be measured in dollars and cents, one thing is sure: Had Irene been sent to a nursing home, and had Al and Becky gone to group homes or the institution, it would have cost thousands of dollars more than the amount expended now.

Later Becky was moved to a group home because of behavior problems. But she has been progressing so well that she now stays overnight on weekends and holidays with her mother and brother. If her progress continues, she soon will be living with them again.

An interesting sidelight: Irene and her children began attending the Congregational Baptist Church with Alice and her family. And the Cissells, touched by the warmth of this larger circle of friends, became members—the only white members in the congregation. Now the pastor, his wife, and members of the congregation drop in, too, providing extra emotional and spiritual support.

During my visit, Al returned home from shopping. The young man with red hair and a wide smile produced a surprise for his mother. He had purchased a mantel clock—something she had been wanting for a long time. Al showed her the mark-down price and the receipt, letting her know he had acquired a great bargain.

While the rest of us watched, Al looked with gentleness and concern at his mom.

"You are a good son," she said, smiling up at him. "I'm lucky."

# 25 - Mealtimes: Great Times for Friends

Mealtimes can be perfunctory hurry-up affairs, or they can be times for the deepest and richest messages one human being can communicate to another. All major religions celebrate holy feasts and holy communions—the breaking of bread on special days—to emphasize the highest values of their faith. I believe that if complete love and understanding ever came to everyone in the world, each mealtime would be a holy Communion.

The happiest times with friends often takes place at mealtimes. We . . .

— feel comradeship and belonging
— relax and become less defensive
— share on many levels
— laugh and feel joyful
— communicate in many ways with voice, eyes, body
— are accepted exactly as we are
— are glad we are who we are
— make choices
— have all the time we need
— heighten all our senses
— and finally, feel full, satisfied and relaxed.

We all have enjoyed human communions like that. Some of them went on for hours. And yet, not so long ago, many people thought mealtimes for persons with severe disabilities were not all that important. They were dribble-chin affairs that helpers tried to get through as fast as they could. Time-motion studies in institutions showed that the average

mealtime on some wards took as little as 4.8 minutes per person! (Perske, 1977, p. xvi).

Many of us have vivid memories of working in residential settings for citizens with severe disabilities when the death rate was higher than 10 percent per year. In those earlier days, too many people choked on their food or died because of aspiration pneumonia caused by insensitive and archaic mealtime practices. Today we know better.

Now we can expect to see people with the severest disabilities and their friends in the finest restaurants. Fred Markham feels sure of it. Markham, an accomplished writer, struggles to overcome erratic muscle movements. In 1977, he observed:

Most of the audiences I have had at restaurants have been sympathetic and willing to understand. People are basically good; they just need to be educated sometimes. Waiters are almost always kind people, and so are the restaurant proprietors whose environments are sometimes unintentionally left in disarray by persons with handicaps. But there are some people, it seems, who still need further understanding. And it is for the benefit of these people—as well as for me—that I will continue to dine out and will be ready to bear up under any situation in which the maitre d' calls to the help, "Guess who's coming for dinner?"

(Markham, p. 16)

**Summer support worker Stacy James with Kurt Long at Brown's Bay YM-YWCA Camp, Brockville, Ontario**

# 26 - Teens Get Summer Jobs Building Friendship Networks

Not all adults—but some—still hold a dark-ages belief that youngsters with disabilities must be protected from other youngsters. They seem ready at the very mention of kids who "aren't normal" to recall a lurid time when a gang of youngsters circled a kid with an obvious vulnerability and jeered and laughed the child into a sobbing heap on the ground . . . or threw stones . . . or chased.

Today, however, kids who demean those with disabilities are a minority. Most young people—if given the chance and a little guidance—can relate to people with disabilities more helpfully than do many adults.

. . . . .

*Brockville, Ontario*—Every summer for the past three years, more than fifty vacationing high school students, and a few collegians, are hired to work in one of two interesting programs. Some are paired with children who have disabilities, and spend the summer as their personal *support workers* in parks or in recreation and day programs throughout the area. Others are paired with teenagers who have disabilities and become their *job coaches*. In both cases, each couple becomes a team for the summer, working or having fun together during the day and going places in the community during the evening hours. The outcome? The two persons in each couple provide for each other one of the richest, most memorable summer work experiences.

The Brockville and District Association for Community Involvement designed these ingenious schemes. This small group of professionals seems to thrive on dreaming up situations where persons with disabilities and so-called normal people can discover, help, and value one another. The remarkable thing about this association is that it makes use of ordinary people and tried-and-true resources that have been available in the neighborhoods for years.

Some government officials and private persons have been so moved by what they've observed the students doing these past three years, there has been no great problem obtaining financial support for the programs —especially paychecks to the "normal" teenagers for their efforts.

In the work programs, each couple works on a single job somewhere in the Greater Brockville district. They may go to a bakery, a grocery store, a restaurant, a hospital, a nursing home, a car wash, or a lumber yard. They do landscaping, house cleaning, boat washing, or anything else two teenagers can dream up to earn a single paycheck. While the persons with the disabilities receive the paychecks from the businesses, the job coaches work side by side with them until they can perform the job alone.

Then comes a priceless result. For the rest of the summer, the job coaches develop subtle ways of helping others at the workplaces understand and befriend their partners. They become public-attitude change experts.

The job coaches' creative juices are kept at a peak when they come together from all over the district to share experiences at weekly group meetings—the only times they are together. Here the coaches report on the "winner" things that have happened to them and their partners. But they share the low points, too. And when a job coach is really having a tough time, the others try to think of new things to try. In doing so, they gain experience as the solvers of real human problems.

The job coaches know they are being watched by others in the workplace. When they exhibit kindness and stability with their partner, the other employees often notice and learn from it. The coaches become models that the others often try to copy.

After-hours activities usually begin with visits to each other's houses for snacks, dinners, and TV watching. As the summer progresses, they start showing up at teenage hangouts, and later they find themselves going places and doing things they never dreamed possible when they first met.

"The beauty of it all," said Ruth Martell, coordinator of the work programs, "is that everything they do is *natural*. These young people merely get to the right place at the right time and—without making any big deal about anything—they connect their friend with the job, and with co-workers, and with other friends. I'm always amazed at the number of young people [with disabilities] who hang onto the jobs after their coaches pull away at the end of the summer."

. . . . .

The programs in which teenagers are paired with smaller children are just as spirited and fruitful. In these cases, however, the couples move into day camps or parks-and-recreation programs instead of jobs at places of business.

Camp counselors and recreation coordinators are usually thrilled to have one more "big" person as an added support worker—one who works without being placed on the already meager payroll.

All the modeling, helping, and reinforcing activities one observes in the work programs are tailor-made for children's settings. And again, one of the major goals is the building of circles of friends around kids with disabilities.

"I love working with these young people," said Sandy Gray, coordinator of the children's programs. "Once you get a teenager interested in the life of one child, and you do some preliminary direction pointing, you can often sit back and watch with amazement. The teenagers amaze you . . . and so does the progress of the child with the challenging problems."

# 27 - Friends Never Feel They Must Fix You

Somehow, when you don't qualify as "normal," you often become the center of a wide array of interventions with words such as these attached to them:

teach
guide
heal
shape
correct
modify
supervise
discipline
prepare
persuade
monitor
coach
evaluate
instruct
manage
enlighten
direct
train
drill
advise
order
control

After an overfull schedule of such relationships, try to sense how you might feel if you suddenly found a friend who

- became attracted to you exactly as you are
- just liked being with you
- and never—repeat *never*—felt the need to fix you.

Quita Lewis and Jason Hickey

# 28 - What's the Big Deal?

Healthy attitude changes are interesting to watch. And the people who work to bring them about develop super commitments. They expend enormous amounts of energy and work long hours each day, sometimes for years. They sweat and anguish, wondering if the day will ever come when people will see the light. But after it happens, the change seems so right and so natural that folks look back and wonder why it took so long.

In a decent society, everyone will see friendships between people with disabilities and so-called normals as right and natural. As for those who already experience such relationships, it has already happened. And when people question them about their togetherness, they wonder why others think it's such a big deal.

. . . . .

*Louisville, Kentucky*—With tight-faced seriousness, Quita Lewis made it plain that she and her friend Jason Hickey of Hawthorne Elementary School had no time for a stranger in the hall taking pictures.

Quita:  "Hey man, we can't stop. If we're late for class, we'll both be in trouble."

Jason nodded in agreement.

Stranger:  "There are lots of kids in the halls yet. It'll just take a second."
Quita:  "Awww. Why do you guys keep coming around with cameras? What's so great?"
Stranger:  "Well, it's a neat school. And you are neat kids. . . . C'mon, just one shot?"
Quita:  "Oh, all right. But make it quick."

She propped an elbow on the chair and Jason stared straight into the camera, both still looking as if they had plums in their mouths.

Stranger:  "Good. Now do you suppose . . . you can sneak in a little smile?"

They smiled.
Click.

Then little Ms. Responsibility and Mr. All-business suddenly did an eyes front and whizzed past the cameraman without giving him another glance.

# 29 - Three Friends Give a Single Speech

Tom Houlihan, Tom Miller, and Ollie Webb

*Pierre, South Dakota*—One of the most memorable speeches I've ever heard was delivered April 10, 1981, at a state convocation for special-education teachers, human-service workers, and parents of persons with developmental disabilities. The topic: Helping Persons with Disabilities to Speak for Themselves. At times the audience broke into unabashed laughter. At other times they became breathlessly silent. Some shed tears.

That speech, describing poignant human situations and pithy new directions, wasn't given by just one person. It was masterfully delivered by three people standing side by side, relaxed and in tune with one another. Every word added to its power and direction.

But most important, it was clear to everyone in the audience that these three people from Omaha, Nebraska, really liked—even loved—one another.

Ollie Webb spent her early childhood and youth at Beatrice State Developmental Center before she was discharged in 1968 to work in an Omaha, Nebraska, nursing home for her food, keep, and a little spending money. Then after learning to speak for herself, and with the help of a network of caring people, Ollie became, and is still, an employee of Omaha's prestigious Field Club. She now owns her own home and serves as a leader in Nebraska's People First movement.

Tom Houlihan never lived in an institution. He grew up in a caring family in the days when no services or opportunities were available for those labeled as Down Syndrome. Although much of his early treatment by society was grim, Tom manages to laugh about what used to happen. He has been a longtime employee of the St. Vincent de Paul Society, lives in his own apartment, and like Ollie, he spearheaded the Nebraska People First movement.

At the time of their speech in 1981, Tom Miller was a human-service employee who had been working with Ollie and Tom for more than ten years.

"Our speaking together is really fun," Miller said. "We sit down beforehand and they tell me the topics they want to raise, and I agree to be their springboard. Once you get Tom and Ollie primed, they take off on their own. They are beautiful . . . so relaxed, so thoughtful. I've come to like them very much."

Although they were remarkable friends, I couldn't help wondering if their closeness would continue if Tom were not a salaried worker in the field.

After seven years, my curiosity got the best of me. I decided to find out.

. . . . .

*Omaha, Nebraska*—Today Miller no longer works in the field of developmental disabilities. But he, Webb, and Houlihan remain as close as they've always been.

"Today, I'm with Tom [Houlihan] more than any other friend," said Miller. They meet for lunches or beers. They go to movies. And ever since Miller began working on his house, Houlihan comes over to help.

According to Miller, his feelings for Houlihan stem from "our being able to share deeply with each other. When I've had it tough, it's natural for me to get with Tom. He listens. He cares. And I try to do the same with him. Even when I moved to Grand Island [Nebraska] for a while, we kept up our contacts. Tom is a great one for sending cards and calling long distance.

"As for Ollie," Miller continued, "every time she sees me, she comes with hugs and kisses and calls me her big brother. She makes you feel worth something." According to Miller, when Ollie has personal problems, she also heads for Tom.

I asked Miller what made them so close. "It's the chemistry," he said. "When I see them at a meeting, I naturally gravitate toward them. It feels so good to be with them . . . the laughing . . . the joking . . . the caring and all. After all, we go back lots of years. . . . There's no doubt in my mind—we will be friends for life."

# 30 - Federal Law Makes Friendships More Likely?

The year 1976 marked the 200th birthday of our country. Any maybe—just maybe—it marked the beginning of numerous friendships between children with disabilities and "regular" students.

That year, the United States government mandated that all state plans for Public Law 94-142 (Education for All Handicapped Act) be in operation by October 1976.

The law, of course, did not call for active friendships. Friendships cannot be mandated.

But, it called for a full-service public school education for children, regardless of their disability, and it spelled out its purposes in minute detail. So much of it inspired many administrators to work for the day when all kids can be educated under the same neighborhood school roof.

. . . . .

Martha Perske attempted to reflect this fresh togetherness in the adjacent montage. When she was commissioned to do the cover for the September 1976 issue of *Early Years*, the national professional magazine for teachers (now known as *Teaching PreK–8*), she was asked to "draw a number of children's faces, all eager to begin school again in September."

She did just that. But in the center of the montage, she drew the face of a child with Down Syndrome, as a signal that "Hey! I'm in school this year, too!"

The drawing was submitted without even mentioning the blond child. After all, the law was the law, and the schoolkids are just schoolkids.

But after the magazine came out, letters commenting on the cover began to pour into the *Early Years* editorial offices.

"Never before has one of our magazine covers drawn so many positive comments," said Pat Broderick, editorial director. Later the magazine sold the cover as a poster. All this may go to show that . . .

- sometimes we focus so much on resistances, we fail to recognize acceptances.
- real friendships can begin only after people meet face to face.

Kimberly Silas and Piper Powell

# 31 - Neighborhood Friends Abound for Piper

Charles Silberman, in *Crisis in the Classroom*, declares out that the neighborhood teaches kids as much as the schools do—or should:

From Plato to Rousseau to Jefferson to the early John Dewey, as Lawrence A. Cremin points out in *The Genius of American Education*, almost everybody who wrote about education took it for granted that it is the community and the culture—what the ancient Greeks called *paideia*—that educates. The contemporary American is educated by his *paideia* no less than the Athenian was by his (p. 5).

. . . . .

*Atlanta, Georgia*—Neighborhood friends abound for Piper Powell. She met most of them as a regular student at Morningside Elementary School. And if you went looking for Piper after school or on the weekends, there's a good chance you'd find her chatting with one of her friends on the telephone, talking about what happened at school or making plans for the next day.

Shopping, movies, birthday parties, going out for pizza, are everyday events Piper and her friends enjoy together. Her friends help her with schoolwork. They jump rope together, play "four square" (the absolute *best* ballgame), and in general have a blast, giggling and sharing third-grade secrets.

Getting to sit by Piper in the auditorium and at lunch and helping her with her work is so popular that at times lists have had to be made to keep peace in the classroom. Two of Piper's friends, Kristy Ogden and Kimberly Mackert, say that "school would be mighty boring without Piper."

Typically, Piper would be attending a segregated school for persons with disabilities some distance outside her neighborhood. She would have little everyday face-to-face contact with kids in her neighborhood, kids who are not handicapped, kids who unwittingly are powerful teachers of adaptive behavior.

Piper's parents, Joe and Trisha Powell, know about the power of *paideia*. And they put their faith in just that power—not in segregated services or in professional specialties.

"We feel so strongly about Piper having a full life in her own neighborhood," said Joe Powell. "We are prepared to work hard to see that it happens."

And so they asked that Piper attend her regular neighborhood public school, just as other kids do. Principal Mike Cooper was game to give it a try. The Powells, wanting to give as much support as necessary, hired a tutor, Betsy Deeter, who goes to class with Piper. Since her regular teachers enthusiastically include Piper in classroom lessons and activities, and many of Piper's peers serve as educational helpers, Deeter has time to develop materials to modify curriculum when necessary and to concentrate with Piper on basic academic skill acquisition. Deeter also sees as part of her role the promotion of the friendships that are so important to Piper now, and in the future.

"During the school year I've seen some interesting changes," said Carolyn Hinske, one of Piper's teachers. "The children have really adjusted to each other. Some who first had been uncertain about Piper have become good friends. And now I see a calmness in Piper, an ability to concentrate better. And when she does something well, she shows great pride in herself."

Hinske saw standards and modeling as the key: "I'm a tough teacher from the old school. I expect *all* my students to behave well. And Piper lives up to those standards. But she also copies the behavior of the other children. If she attended a class where everyone had Down Syndrome, she would have been mimicking them."

As for the other students, Hinske added, "I've observed the growing naturalness, the kindness, and the helpfulness of Kimberly Silas, who sits next to Piper. The same can be said about the others sitting close to her. And I can tell you these children are growing because they *know* they are helping someone else. They feel good about it. And that's a feeling many students don't get in their classes."

Said principal Mike Cooper, "I see it as a good way to help all our kids to be more accepting of others, whether they have exceptionalities or not. If I had to do it all over again, I'd do it. It'll be exciting to see how it all comes out."

# 32 - "Just Friends" Makes the News

Dan Piper and Jim Mollison

I remember the days when newspapers said little about people with disabilities until they got into trouble. Then the headlines screamed out their problems in lurid detail. Today many reporters describe disabilities in less negative terms, and some should be commended for beginning to present the bright, community-enriching side of people who have disabilities.

*Ankeny, Iowa*—The April 26, 1987, issue of the *Des Moines Register* contained a page-one story about the friendship between Dan Piper and Jim Mollison, two students at Nevelyn Junior High. Reporter Ken Fuson did a beautiful job, but more folks need to know about Dan and Jim:

- They first saw each other in the halls when both were seventh-graders. Jim was a "reg" and Dan was in "special ed." They said Hi to each other.
- Jim got to know Dan better after asking Dan's teacher if he could help out in the special ed class, giving up two study halls daily. He helped with spelling, reading, counting money, writing letters, and with sports.
- Then on a Sunday morning in February, Jim called Dan and invited him to go bowling. Dan's parents were flabbergasted. "Do you know what that meant to us?" Dan's mother said. "That never happened before. This wasn't a friend of the family. This was a friend he made on his own!"
- Jim worked long hours coaching Dan in the long jump and in throwing a softball.
- Many observers commented on the healthy give-and-take that always seemed to go on between the two.
- Dan became a staunch rooter for Jim, who played on the football and baseball teams, and Dan increased his rooting when he became student manager of the football team.
- Dan and Jim found lots of things to do together—bowling, swimming, bike riding, roller skating, Coke drinking, hang-

ing out at the mall, and going to see the Monkees in Des Moines.
- When Dan performed in a skit with six others at the Summerfest—portraying John Travolta and the T-Birds—Jim was in the stands, cheering for his friend.

These activities were gleaned from Fuson's article and from talking to others who know Dan and Jim. We managed to gather several photographs of the pair together, from which the montage was created, giving you a larger, richer picture of the young men.

And for helping you feel how these two fit together so well, here are some words direct from reporter Fuson:

They are an odd couple. Mollison is a foot taller. Piper has the deeper voice.

Mollison walks through the halls quietly; Piper bounces along, collecting greetings.

In other ways, though, they are nearly identical, their sense of humor tuned to the same dial:

| | |
|---|---|
| Jim: | "Did you take that Pepsi Challenge?' |
| Dan: | "Me? Yes." |
| Jim: | "What did you pick?" |
| Dan: | "The Monkees." |
| Jim: | "Come on. Which one?" |
| Dan: | "Diet Mountain Dew." |
| Jim: | "I don't think there is one. Are you running a little slow today?" |
| Dan: | "No, are you?" |

*Afterthoughts:*
Many newspapers are writing about friendships like this nowadays, but will they continue? Perhaps for a time . . . but not forever. And during a telephone visit, Jim Mollison provided me with a possible reason.

"What do you get out of the friendship?" I asked.

There was a long silence, making me feel I

had asked a question that was slightly odd.

Then he spoke: "Gee, I don't know. I just do it because I like to. Hey, it's not work. We're just friends."

Jim's statement got me thinking:

—Friendships are natural things.
—Jim saw this friendship as natural.
—Will stories like this someday become so commonplace they won't be newsworthy?

Yvette Mollot and Ruth Harper of Winnipeg, Manitoba, enjoy each other's company.

# 33 - John O'Brien Digs Good Roots

*Decatur, Georgia*—While we attempted to capture stories, ideas, and images from real people, a friend, John O'Brien, kept in touch with us.

He decided to go after *friendship* by another route—by "climbing down an etymology ladder" to discover what the word meant to people in other ages. His findings:

## A NOTE ON THE LINGUISTIC ROOTS OF FRIENDSHIP

If you want to stand up for a word, it's good to know how deep its roots go, where it comes from, and what its relations are. Renewing the meaning of old words brings power and richness to life. Deep roots connect the friends whose stories you tell in your book with some of humankind's highest hopes and most powerful words.

The actions captured in your stories and pictures renew the word *friend*. A brief look at its origins helps to make clear what we bring to life when we stand up for *friendship*. However flimsy *just friends* may seem in a high-tech world, it can draw upon the power of the ages.

*Friend* is a word as old as written English. *The Oxford English Dictionary* notes that more than a thousand years ago, the poet sang of Beowulf, who fought the monsters that threatened Hrothgar's household, because Beowulf was Hrothgar's friend: *one joined to another in mutual benevolence and intimacy*.

At its beginning, the word *friend* was created by a contraction of the old English verb *frijon* which means *to love* (Partridge).

That word in turn arose from the ancient Indo-European root *prai* which means *beloved, precious, at peace with,* and *free* (Shipley). Powerful ancestors indeed.

The roots of the word *friend* illuminate the source of some of our most prized human qualities (Benveniste). *Liberty* and *citizenship* arise linguistically and politically from groups of people who call one another friends. Freedom, however, does not derive from words that speak of being free of something, but from words that speak of belonging to a *circle of friends*. And it is ties of *affection* and *belonging* that lie at the linguistic roots of oneself. At root, *a person discovers self only among friends*.

. . . . .

Although John's note ended here, his interest in the linguistic roots of *friendship* continued. Five months later, he contacted me. Reading an original French version of *Indio-European Language and Society* by Benveniste, he discovered that in much earlier days, people of privilege could not be friends with . . .

— people having no property
— people of low social status
— women
— foreigners

So when we call another *friend*, we may be helping that person to be liberated from oppressive restrictions. At the same time, we can break out of a narrow, closed circle of privilege.

# 34 - An Open Letter to Robert Williams

You provided some of the reasons Martha and I wanted to do this book:

- Eleven years ago, you and I sat together at a government hearing in Hartford, Connecticut. You had your board with the alphabet and words on it, and you began to spell sentences with your finger. Right then, you became more interesting to me than all the oral garbage that filled the air that day. You—with that educated finger—cut through the verbiage to the central issues and the real right or wrong of them. Next came meetings in Washington, D.C., where I spied you on the fringe of the crowd, quietly waiting until all the "talkers" had left. Then, with your communication board between us, I learned to slow down, to watch, to listen, and to be enlightened and feel strangely relaxed.

- You invited me to spend evenings and days off with you in your apartment in Washington, and I remember my first full day with you. I learned of your knowledge and respect for Abraham Lincoln . . . Franklin D. Roosevelt . . . Martin Luther King, Jr. . . . the civil rights movement . . . and the songs of the 1960s. From that time on, you and your apartment became a gold mine of ideas, world views, and laughter.

- I became acquainted with your friends. And though I don't see them as often as you do, I feel close to John, Lissa, Sandy, Frank, Tony, Mike, Debbie, Dottie, Margaret, and Karen—after hearing you talk about them and seeing them through your eyes.

- Small wonder that our little dog enjoys sitting on your lap and being hugged—and that Ali, your cat, comes out from her hiding place to be close to you. Martha once said, "I could never live with a person who was mean to little furry creatures," and that moved me to practice kindness. But you are naturally kind.

- Although communication takes time, each sentence comes across like a shortstop's throw—nothing wasted, right on target. You refuse to gild the lily with fancy modifiers. You make your verbs work! And I chuckle to myself when well-meaning professionals use *fifty* sentences to convince you that your communication would be more efficient if you used one of the recently manufactured contraptions. If they ever relaxed and slowed down and really *listened* to your

Robert Williams, with Jake Perske

choice few sentences, they'd have cause to think about what they have been missing.

- I recall your poise when able-bodied persons caused you anguish—the cab driver who pulled up to us on Virginia Avenue, then sped away; the airline employee in Minneapolis who told you (a frequent flyer) that you should never fly alone; the United States Supreme Court building, when access to an inside ramp was denied you and some of us carried your electric vehicle, piece by piece, to the top steps so you could attend an important hearing. All your life you have suffered at the hands of unfeeling people.

- Once you criticized me for writing a fictional piece in which I attacked a mother for not accepting a son with a disability. You quickly let me know that if you hadn't been born to a large family with grandparents, aunts and uncles, and "a slew of cousins all within hollering distance"—you would have been languishing on a mat in a large institution ten miles from your home. After I got to know your family, I understood what you meant.

- I've watched you take careful aim at the individuals and bureaucracies who harmed one of your "brothers or sisters." When one organization televised their breakthroughs with a woman who has severe cerebral palsy—then allowed her to regress and be moved to a nursing home when the project was over—your well-aimed sentences helped foster a solution instead of a cover-up. When the *Washington Post* published William Buckley's column in which he claimed that Jim Dickson—because of his absence of sight—was foolish to sail his sloop to Bermuda alone (August 12, 1987), you defended Dickson's ingenuity, insight, and daring (August 24, 1987).

- As a court-appointed monitor who oversees the transfer of people from Forest Haven, a District of Columbia institution, into the community, your commitment is obvious. And all who know you are especially aware of your single-minded concern for "my folks"—those people with whom you would have been matmates if it hadn't been for your family.

- You make no bones about the need for people with disabilities to speak for themselves. So it's understandable that most of our recent liveliest conversations have centered on . . .

— how the student body of Gallaudet University protested vigorously until a president who also has a hearing impairment was chosen

— how Christopher Nolan's *Under the Eye of the Clock* has opened fresh vistas for you and your "brothers and sisters"

— our viewing of *Gaby: A True Story* at a Washington theater and the way Gabrielle Brimmer's story can affect the lives of hundreds of people with cerebral palsy

— your intent to network with the Nolans and the Brimmers of the world

— your intense interest in the self-advocacy organizations springing up across the continent.

. . . . .

I always seem to have unfinished business with you because I'm usually fifty miles down the road before many of the things you tried to tell me finally penetrate my skull.

I like having unfinished business with you.

Becky Saunders, Stephanie Rogers, and Dawn Marie Hanna of Westport, Ontario, spent most of the daylight hours of their summer vacation together as close friends. The mother of the girl with the disability said, "She has been integrated into the community since nursery school. She has transcended the isolation experienced by many others."

# 35 - Afterword

After spending most of my working life in one mechanism or another of The Great American Human Service Machine, I've witnessed an interesting phenomenon. Years ago, all components of The Machine functioned like a giant multicannister vacuum sweeper with a long hose. It moved through neighborhoods, looking for those who didn't seem . . . normal. And when it found such persons, it labeled and classified them, convinced family and friends that they were helpless, and determined which canister should receive the labeled ones. Then it sucked them out of the community.

But times changed.

A few human-service workers dared to look past the labels and tried to think themselves into the skins of the people they served. They discovered people who, in spite of the labels they had been given, longed to be liberated from an awful loneliness, to be loved and valued, to be accomplished in something—the very same longings the rest of us possess.

So those human-service workers, so moved by what they observed, tended less and less to be the diagnosis-and-deposit functionaries they had been trained to be. They worked out mechanisms that tried to help the people they served achieve the richest life possible.

The Machine slowly made a turnaround. It placed people back into their neighborhoods. It tried, however, to put people back more carefully than it had taken them out. It developed all kinds of community living programs. And it struggled to keep others with disabilities from ever having to leave their neighborhoods.

But times changed again.

A more sensitive and responsive machine rediscovered the value and power of the family. It saw that families can do things the vacuum sweeper Machine could never do. And so it developed family support programs.

Then times changed again.

Human-service workers gradually learned that even with billions of dollars in grants, even with the most brilliant technologies, even with leading-edge community programs, even with the kindest family-support services possible—something was still missing. People needed friends. Nobody can be fully present or participate in a neighborhood without them.

And so human-service workers have come to believe that ordinary citizens have something to offer people with disabilities which they—even with all their training—cannot provide.

As people take to each other, persons with disabilities have been able to contribute their own unique richness to their friends and to the surrounding neighborhoods as well. Therefore I believe that friendships with people who have disabilities can provide an explosion of fresh values and directions which this confused, misdirected world needs now as never before.

So times may change again!

Amber Beth Langevin, Fairfield, Ohio, someone's future valued friend

# References

Benveniste, Emile. *Indo-European Language and Society*. Coral Gables: University of Miami Press, 1973.

Cousins, Norman. "Prophesy and Pessimism." *Saturday Review. World.* August 24, 1974.

Daniel, Carolyn. "Wanted: Just One Friend." *Parent to Parent*, April 1987 (Tri-State Organized Coalition for Persons with Disabilities).

DeBevoise, Wynn. "Mainstreaming Can Benefit the Nonhandicapped, Too." *Principal*, March 1986.

De Saint Exupery, Antoine. *The Little Prince*. New York: Harcourt Brace Jovanovich, 1943.

ENCOR. *Why Be Friends*. Omaha: Eastern Nebraska Community Office of Retardation, 1972.

*Gaby—A True Story*. Los Angeles: Tri-Star Pictures, 1987.

Howe, Harold II. "Report to the President of the United States from the Chairman of the White House Conference on Education, August 1, 2024." *Saturday Review. World*, August 24, 1974.

Lewis, C. S. *The Four Loves*. New York: Harcourt Brace Jovanovich, 1971.

Markham, Fred. "On Eating Out: A Severely Handicapped Person's Point of View." *Mealtimes for Persons with Severe Handicaps*, ed. Robert Perske; Andrew Clifton; Barbara McLean; and Jean Stein. Baltimore: Paul H. Brookes Publishing Co., 1977.

Nolan, Christopher. *Under the Eye of the Clock*. New York: St. Martin's Press, 1987.

Partridge, Eric. *Origins: A Short Etymological Dictionary of Modern English*. New York: Crown Publishers, 1983.

Perske, Robert. "A Gentle Call to Revolution." *Mealtimes for Persons with Severe Handicaps*, ed. Perske et al., 1977.

————. *Report to the President: Mental Retardation, the Leading Edge—Service Programs That Work*. Washington, D. C.: President's Committee on Mental Retardation, 1978.

Pogrebin, Letty Cottin. *Among Friends: Who We Like, Why We Like Them, and What We Do with Them*. New York: McGraw-Hill, 1987.

RTC/IL. *Guidelines for Reporting and Writing About People with Disabilities*. Lawrence, Kan.: Research and Training Center on Independent Living, BCR/3111, University of Kansas, 1987.

Rubin, Lillian. *Just Friends: The Role of Friendship in Our Lives*. New York: Harper & Row, 1985.

Smith, Fred. "What About Me?" *Dialect*, February 1987 (Saskatoon: Saskatchewan Association for the Mentally Retarded).

Schaefer, Nicola. *Does She Know She's There?* Garden City, N. Y.: Doubleday, 1978.

Shipley, Joseph. *The Origins of English Words: A Discursive Dictionary of Indo-European Roots*. Baltimore: Johns Hopkins Press, 1984.

Silberman, Charles E. *Crisis in the Classroom: The Remaking of Education*. New York: Random House, 1970.

Stephenson, Wendy. *Roxene*. Calgary: Detselig Enterprises, 1983.

Walt Disney Productions. "The Ugly Duckling." *Tales of Jiminy Cricket*, Episode 4. New York: Cathedral Films, 1959.

Weiss, Robert S. "Loneliness: What We Know About It and What We Might Do About It." *Preventing the Harmful Consequences of Severe and Persistent Loneliness.*, ed. L. A. Peplow and S. E. Goldston. Rockville, Md.: National Institute of Mental Health, 1982.

Whitehead, Alfred North. *Science and the Modern World*. New York: The MacMillan Co., 1957.

Kelly Garrison of Apple Valley, Minnesota, someone's future valued friend